LUTTRELL SOCIETY REPRINTS No. 21

THE LIFE OF SETH
Lord Bishop of Salisbury

THE
LIFE OF SETH
Lord Bishop of Salisbury

By WALTER POPE

Edited by J. B. BAMBOROUGH

OXFORD,
Published for the Luttrell Society
by Basil Blackwell
MCMLXI

Printed in Great Britain for BASIL BLACKWELL & MOTT, LTD.
by A. R. MOWBRAY & CO. LIMITED in the City of Oxford
and bound at the KEMP HALL BINDERY

CONTENTS

The copy used for this reprint is that belonging to Wadham College, by kind permission of the Librarian.

INTRODUCTION

WALTER POPE was born in the parish of Fawsley in Northampton-shire. His mother was a daughter of the Puritan divine John Dod, who was Rector of Fawsley from 1624 until his death in 1645; by a previous marriage she was the mother of John Wilkins. There is no record of Pope's birth, but the likelihood is that it was between 1625 and 1630. He was edu-cated at Westminster School, where one of his school-fellows was the controversialist Edward Bagshaw, who is the 'Ned' referred to in Chapter VI of Pope's *Life of Seth Ward*. From Westminster he went as a scholar to Trinity College, Cambridge, where he was admitted in June 1645; thence he migrated in 1648 to Oxford, having been appointed by the Parliamentary Visitors to a scholarship at Wadham, of which college his half-brother became Warden in the same year.[1] He took his B.A. on 6 July 1649 and was appointed to a Fellowship by the Committee for the Reformation of the

[1] The date of his appointment is given in the Register of the Visitors (now in the Bodleian) as Oct. 16, 1648. There is no record of his admission, but the records of the College were very badly kept for the whole of Wilkins's Wardenship.

Universities on 3 July 1651; he was admitted as a Fellow on 9 July, and took his
M.A. on the following day. He was Bursar
of the College in 1655 and again in 1657,
and Sub-warden in 1658.

He was lucky in his College. Wadham
was still a young foundation, and a comparatively small and poor Society, and had
suffered badly in the early days of the
Visitation, when a high proportion of its
Fellows and Scholars had been extruded for
non-compliance. Yet this in the long run
proved an advantage, for the vacant places
were filled by men—among them Pope
himself—who were acceptable to the Visitors, and consequently there was little
further trouble; Wadham was one of the
first Colleges to have restored to it (in 1651)
the right to elect its own Fellows and
Scholars. Above all the College was fortunate in having Wilkins as its head, for, as
Pope says, he attracted many distinguished
men to it. Wren became a Fellow-Com-
moner in 1649; Ward and Rooke Fellow-
Commoners in 1650, and Sprat, the historian of the Royal Society, matriculated as
a commoner in 1651. From about 1652
until 1659, when Wilkins went to Cambridge as Master of Trinity College, the

'Philosophical Society', composed of the Oxford members of the group which was later to become the Royal Society, met regularly in the Warden's lodgings. Nor was the College filled only with the 'virtuosi'; in Pope's time it had among its members two of the most notorious of the rakes of the Restoration—Charles Sedley, and John Wilmot Earl of Rochester. Pope's *Life of Ward* is very much of a Wadham product; not only is it written by one member of the College about another, but the John Wyndham to whom it is dedicated was descended from a sister of Nicholas Wadham, Founder of the College.[1]

Pope was elected Junior Proctor of the University on 21 April 1658 the year of the 'Controversie concerning Caps and Hoods', which he records in the sixth chapter of his *Life of Ward*. Apparently he did not serve out his year of office, being granted leave to travel abroad, or, as Wood says with his usual waspishness,

> ... to be absent for the avoiding the making of a speech, which he was to do before he resigned up his office.[2]

[1] John Wyndham, who represented Salisbury in the Parliament of 1685, was the founder's great-grand-nephew. See the Pedigree of Wadham in Sir Thomas Jackson's History of the College (1893).

[2] *Athenae Oxonienses*, ed. Bliss (1820), IV, 724.

On 10 September 1659 he wrote to Boyle
from Paris, apologizing for having little of
scientific interest to report, adding

> ... I am very much ashamed to tell you,
> that I have spent most of my leisure time
> reading romances, which we hire like horses,
> and monsieur *Corneille's* plays, and visiting
> the eminent places in and about this city.

but promising to send details of any other
curiosities he comes across.[1] He was back
in Oxford later in September 1659, however, for he signed the Convention Book
when Wilkins resigned as Warden. On
6 December 1661 he was elected Dean of
the College for the ensuing twelve months,
and on 12 September 1661 he received
the degree of Doctor of Medicine 'favore
Cancellarii'. On 28 January 1662 he was
granted leave of absence until February
16th, and on June 27th of the same year
was removed from his Fellowship because
the Statutes prevented him from holding it
in conjunction with the Professorship of
Astronomy at Gresham College, to which
he had been appointed on 8 March 1661
in succession to Christopher Wren.[2] Perhaps he was already living in London, for

[1] *The Works of the Hon. Robert Boyle* (1744), Vol. V, p. 631.
[2] Who had succeeded Ward as Savilian Professor of Astronomy in Oxford.

he had been admitted to the Royal Society
(not yet, of course, incorporated) on 22
May 1661 and attended some of its
meetings.[1]

He was an active member of the Society
in its early days. On 13 June 1661 he was
asked to 'procure the experiment of breaking pebbles with the hand', and on October
16th performed the experiment before the
Society 'which succeeded very well';[2] in
June 1662 he and others were 'desired to
try the variation of the needle at Whitehall',
and on July 9th of the same year he and
Doctor (Matthew) Wren were desired to
consider the observations of Jupiter's satellites which (as he notes in the *Life of Ward*)
Lawrence Rooke had left incomplete at his
death in the preceding month.[3]

In 1663 and 1664 he travelled on the
Continent, apparently going as tutor to
Evelyn's nephew George;[4] in April 1664
he wrote to Wilkins from Rome, in August
1664 from Padua and in September from
Venice—all letters describing matters of
scientific interest.[5] He is not recorded as
attending meetings of the Royal Society

[1] Birch, *History of the Royal Society of London* (1756),
Vol. I, p. 25.   [2] Ibid., pp. 29, 50.   [3] Ibid., pp. 85, 88.
[4] Evelyn, *Diary* 4 April 1663 (ed. De Beer, Vol. III, p. 354).
[5] Ward, *Lives of the Professors of Gresham College* (1790),
pp. 112, 115–16.

again until 1666, when he was living in
London; at the Annual Meeting on November 30th of that year he was elected to the
Council of the Society for the ensuing year,
as he was again in November of 1668.

During this time he was carrying out his
duties as Gresham Professor of Astronomy,
as Edward Sherburne testifies, listing in his
'Catalogue of the most eminent Astrologers
Ancient and Modern':

> Doctor WALTER POPE, *Professor of Astronomy*
> in Gresham College; the successor of Sir
> *Christopher Wrenn* and Mr. *Rook*; with whom
> he hath spent much time in observing the
> Motions and Appearances of the Heavens;
> the Result of which he hath delivered in his
> Astronomical Lectures there read, which 'tis
> hoped he may be prevailed to make public
> hereafter.[1]

In fact Pope never published any scientific work, as Wood noticed with mock-
regret; instead he offered as his first publica-
tion, in 1670, *The Memoires of Monsieur Du
Vall: containing the History of his Life and
Death. Whereunto are Annexed His last
Speech and Epitaph.* Wood noted in the
first edition of *Athenae Oxonienses* that this

[1] Appendix (p. 113) to *The Sphere of M. Manilius, made
into an English Poem,* 1675.

was written 'out of pique', adding in a later note (apparently written in 1693) that the famous highwayman

> ... having been a brisk, smart, gay, and handsome fellow, and of about 27 years of age when he was hanged at Tyburn (which was on the 21st of January 1669) did draw the loves of many females in London towards him: Amongst which was the miss of our author Pope, who taking it in great indignation that his person, doctorship and merits, should be so slighted for the sake of an ignorant rogue, he did therefore write the said *Memoirs*, wherein are many satyrical girds against the females.[1]

In fact Pope's motive seems clearly to have been to mock the fuss made over a convicted criminal, and the contemporary craze (which Dryden satirized not long afterwards in *Marriage a la Mode*) for all things French; what little support there is for Wood's story comes from Pope's account of being disowned by his mistress for daring to suggest 'That a French lacquey was not so good as an English gentleman'.[2] The real point of his satire comes out in the 'last

---

[1] *Ath. Ox.*, ed. Bliss, IV, p. 725. The Pindaric Ode, *To the Memory of the Most Renowned Du-Vall*, published in the same year, which Wood believed to be Pope's, appears in fact to be, as its title-page states, by Samuel Butler.

[2] *Memoires of Du-Vall*, p. 18.

speech' he gives the highwayman, addressed
to the Ladies:

> How *mightily* and how *generously* have you
> rewarded my *little* Services? Shall I ever
> forget that *universall Consternation* amongst
> you when I was taken, your *frequent*, your
> *chargeable Visits* to me in *Newgate*, your
> *Shreeks*, your *Swoonings* when I was *con-
> demned*, your *Zealous intercession* and *Impor-
> tunity* for my *Pardon*?
>
> You could not have erected fairer pillars
> of Honour and respect for me, had I been a
> *Hercules*, and could have got *fifty Sons* in a
> night.
>
> It has been the Misfortune of several
> *English* Gentlemen, in the times of the late
> Usurpation, to die at this place upon the
> *Honourablest Occasion* that ever *presented* it-
> self, the indeavouring to restore their *Exil'd
> Sovereign*: *Gentlemen* indeed, who had ven-
> tured their *Lives*, and lost their *Estates* in the
> Service of their Prince; but they all died
> *unlamented* and *uninterceded* for, because
> they were *English*. How much greater there-
> fore is my Obligation, whom you love better
> than your own *Country-men*, better than your
> own *dear Husbands*? Nevertheless, Ladies,
> it does not grieve me, that your Intercession
> for my life proved ineffectual; For now I
> shall die with *little pain*, a *healthful body*, and
> I hope a *prepared mind*. For my Confessor
> has shewed me the Evil of my way, and
> wrought in me a true Repentance; witness

these *tears*, these *unfeigned tears*. Had you prevail'd for my life, I must in gratitude have devoted it wholly to you, which yet would have been but short; for, had you been sound, I should have soon died of a *Consumption*; if otherwise, of the POX.[1]

Pope suggests a way of remedying the ladies' passion for Frenchmen which foreshadows the project of the Academy of Lagado for reconciling the political parties:

I have heard that there is a new invention of Transfusing the bloud of one Animal into another,[2] and that it has been experimented by putting the blood of a Sheep into an English man. I am against that way of experiments, for should we make all *English* men *Sheep*, we should soon be a prey to the *Louure*.

I think I can propose the making that Experiment a more advantageous way. I would have all Gentlemen, who have been a full year, or more, out of *France*, be let blood weekly, or oftner if they can bear it; mark how much they bleed, transfuse so

---

[1] Pp. 14–15.

[2] Pope the scientist is speaking here. In Nov. 1666 the Royal Society had reported to it experiments made in the transfusion of blood from one animal into another, and Pope was appointed one of the 'curators' to experiment further. In Dec. 1666 it was reported that further experiments had been successfully carried out, and 'Dr. Pope moved, that a trial might be made of letting one half the blood of a dog and supplying it with warm milk, or, because milk may coagulate, with a liquid of barley-cream'—not, one would have thought, a profitable line of research. (Birch, *op. cit.*, Vol. I, pp. 125, 133, 134.)

much *French* Lacqueys blood into them, Replenish these last out of the English footmen, for 'tis no matter what become of them. Repeat this Operation *Toties Quoties*, and in process of time you'l find this Event: Either the *English Gentlemen* will be as much belov'd as the *French Lacqueys*; or the *French Lacqueys* as little esteemed as the *English Gentlemen*.[1]

The *Memoires of Du Vall* was a very successful squib; according to a manuscript note by Wood in his own copy,[2] it sold 10,000 copies. Two years later Pope produced a more scholarly work, an edition of the Latin Fables of Gabriel Faerno,[3] and in 1674 another of what Wood calls his 'vain and frivolous things', *The Catholick Ballad*.[4] This, a black-letter broadside, is apparently a riposte to *The Geneva Ballad*, an attack on 'th' Enthusiastick breed' (the phrase is used seven years before *Absalom and Achitophel*) published in the same year. It is hardly more than of moderate satirical force.

Seth Ward was translated from Exeter to Salisbury in 1667 (not 1666 as Pope says),

---

[1] Pp. 20–21.   [2] Bodl. Lib. *Wood* 372.
[3] *Centum Fabulae ex Antiquis Auctoribus Delectae, et a Gabriele Faerno Cremornensi, Carminibus explicatae*, Londini, Impenso H. Brome . . . 1672.
[4] *The Catholic Ballad: or an Invitation to Popery, upon considerable Grounds and Reasons—To the tune of* 88. London: Printed for Henry Brome . . . 1674.

and presumably Pope joined his household then, though he must also have spent some time in Chester; Wilkins appointed him Registrar of that diocese when he became Bishop of Chester in 1668, and he held the office until his death. In 1676 he published *The Salisbury-Ballad*,[1] referred to in the *Life of Ward* as 'The Salisbury Canto'. This is a very rare work. It consists of a large single sheet containing 27 stanzas surrounded by a mass of notes; it begins thus:

O Salisbury People give ear to my Song,
    And attention unto my new Ditty:
For it is in the praise of your River *Avon*,
    Of your Bishop, your Church and your
                         [City.

II

And your Maior and Aldermen all on a row,
    Who govern that [a]watered Mead,
First [b]listen a while, upon your [c]tipto.
    Then carry this home and [d]read.

a The City of New *Sarum* Built in the Bishops Meadow.
b to the Ballad-Singers. *c* In a posture of attention. *d* Here the Poet is in a good humour, and supposes that all of them can read.

Wood, ready as ever to impute base motives to Pope, says of the *Salisbury Ballad*

... This was a satyr written against Seth bishop of Sals. for depriving him of his miss,

---

[1] *The Salisbury-Ballad*. With the learned Commentaries of a Friend to the Authors Memory. London: Printed for Henry Brome, 1676.

which caused a difference between them for a time;[1]

this is based, if anything, on the fifth stanza, which is worth quoting for its own sake:

School-Mistresses fine, to the number of
    Ile call on no Muses but you;   [[h]Nine
Nor no other help to enter my [i]Whelp
    Unless it be [k]bouncing [l]Pru.

[h] Not but that there are a greater number of School-mistresses in the Close, but the Poet hath no need of no more of them than there were Muses. [i] My young barking Muse. *Ma Muse nourrie en Satire.* Boi. [k] that word signifies fat or dancing. [l] A diminutive from *Prudence*, and seems to be put here for any Woman at large only to complete the Ryme, it being a name suitable enough; for most Women are wise, if not cunning: I confess some who pretend to have been intimately acquainted with the Poet in his life-time, are very positive, that this name did not only point out a particular Woman but even the Poets Mistress; but I cannot agree to this, for had it been so, he would have give her a more honourable Epithet.

In the rest of the Ballad Pope refers to the many benefits which the Bishop has brought to Salisbury, most of them mentioned again in his *Life of Ward*—for example, the re-building of the Bishop's Palace and the widening of the river in 1675—and he also celebrates the skill of Turberville, the eye-doctor. The whole poem in fact reads like a versified commentary on the *Life of Ward*, with agreeable additional notes—as when Pope recounts how the men of Old Sarum

[1] *Ath. Oxon.* (ed. Bliss), IV, 725.

came down from their Hill 'That they might have a Mill and water at will', and comments 'At hand for all conveniences, as washing of dishes, drowning of children, etc.'—and in its way it is as good as the *Life*.

Pope's most successful poem, however, and his best-known work, is his 'Wish'. Wood says this was printed in 1684,[1] but the earliest version to survive is in two collections of songs both published in 1685, Henry Playford's *The Theatre of Musick*, and *A Choice Collection of* 180 *Loyal Songs*, edited by N.T(hompson), in both of which it appears (with music) as *The Old Man's Wish*. It was issued separately, as a pamphlet, in 1693,[2] and again in book form in 1697 as *The Wish*, with a dedication to Charles, Lord Clifford. It was very popular, and has reached the dignity of inclusion in *The Oxford Book of Quotations* and *The Oxford Book of* 17th *Century Verse*, but since it is there quoted in the much truncated version printed in Playford, I give it here in full from the edition of 1697, which

[1] Wood also says that Pope tried and failed to get the poem published in Sir Roger L'Estrange's *Observator*. See *Ath. Oxon.* (ed. Bliss), IV, 725, and the *Observator* for 9 Jan. 1685 (Vol. III, No. 126).

[2] *Doctor* POPES WISH. The only Correct and Finished Copy. Never before Printed ... London: Printed for Thomas Horne ... MDCXCIII.

is Pope's final version,[1] but omitting all but
one of the copious notes of that edition:[2]

I

If I live to be old, for I find I go down,
Let this be my Fate. In a Country Town,
May I have a warm House, with a Stone at the
    Gate,
And a cleanly young Girl, to rub my bald Pate.

Chorus.

May I govern my Passion with an absolute
    Sway,
And grow Wiser, and Better, as my Strength
    wears away,
Without Gout, or Stone, by a gentle decay.

II

May my little House stand on the Side of a Hill,
With an easy Descent, to a Mead, and a Mill,
That when I've a mind, I may hear my Boy
    read,
In the Mill, if it rains, if it's dry, in the Mead.
May I govern, &c.

---

[1] There are a good many variants between the different
versions. Thompson's *Loyal Songs* adds a stanza after st. V
which runs:

When the days are grown short, and it Freezes and snows
May I have a Cole fire as high as my Nose;
A fire (which once stirr'd up with a Prong)
Will keep the Room temperate all the night long.

This does not re-appear later, and may be spurious.

[2] These are not so much notes as citations of parallel
passages, from, e.g., Horace, Petrarch, and the Dutch poet
and moralist, Jacob Cats, whom Pope is fond of quoting.
More than once there are several pages of commentary to one
stanza of the poem.

III

Near a shady Grove, and a murmuring Brook,
With the Ocean at Distance, whereupon I may
  look,
With a spacious Plain, without Hedge or Stile,
And an easie Pad-Nag, to ride out a Mile.
May I govern, &c.

IV

With *Horace* and *Petrarch*, and Two or Three
  more
Of the best Wits that reign'd in the Ages before,
With roast Mutton, rather than Ven'son or
  Teal,
And clean, tho' course Linnen at every Meal.
May I govern, &c.

V

With a Pudding on Sundays, with stout hum-
  ming Liquor,
And Remnants of Latin to welcome the Vicar,
With *Monte-Fiascone*, or *Burgundy* Wine
To drink the Kings Health as oft as I dine.
May I govern, &c.

VI

May my Wine be Vermillion, may my Malt-
  drink be pale,
In neither extream, or too mild or too stale,
In lieu of Deserts, Unwholsome and Dear,
Let *Lodi* or *Parmisan* bring up the Rear.
May I govern, &c.

VII

Nor Tory, or Wig, Observator or Trimmer
May I be, nor against the Laws Torrent a
 Swimmer.
May I mind what I speak, what I write, and
 hear read,
But with matters of State ne'er trouble my Head.
May I govern, &c.

VIII

Let the Gods who dispose of every Kings
 Crown,
Whomsoever they please, set up and pull down.
Ile pay the whole Shilling impos'd on my Head
Tho I go without[1] Claret that Night to my Bed.
May I govern, &c.

IX

I'll bleed without grumbling, tho' that Tax
 should appear
As oft as New Moons, or Weeks in a Year,
For why should I let a seditious Word fall?
Since my Lands in *Utopia* pay nothing at all.
May I govern, &c.

X

Tho' I care not for Riches, may I not be so poor,
That the Rich without shame cannot enter my
 Door,
May they court my converse, may they take
 much delight,
My old Stories to hear in a Winters long Night.
May I govern, &c.

---

[1] If that should happen, it would be a shrewd Affliction to
the Poet. (Pope's note.)

XI

My small stock of Wit may I not misapply,
To flatter great men be they never so high,
Nor mispend the few Moments I steal from the
   Grave,
In fawning, or cringing, like a Dog or a Slave.
May I govern, &c.

XII

May none whom I love, to so great Riches rise
As to slight their Acquaintance, and their old
   Friends despise,
So Low or so High, may none of them be,
As to move either Pity, or Envy in me.
May I govern, &c.

XIII

A Friendship I wish for, but alas 'tis in vain,
Joves Store-House is empty and can't it supply,
So firm, that no change of Times, Envy, or
   Gain,
Or Flatt'ry, or Woman, should have Pow'r to
   unty.
May I govern, &c.

XIV

But if Friends prove unfaithful, and Fortune a
   Whore,
Still may I be Virtuous, though I am poor,
My Life then, as useless, may I freely resign,
When no longer I relish, true Wit, and good
   Wine.
May I govern, &c.

XV

To out live my Senses may it not be my Fate,
To be blind, to be deaf, to know nothing at all,
But rather let Death come before 'tis so late,
And while there's some Sap in it, may my Tree
   fall.
May I govern, &c.

XVI

I hope I shall have no occasion to send
For Priests, or Fysicians, till I am so near mine
   End
That I have eat all my Bread, and drunk my
   last Glass,
Let them come then, and set their Seals to my
   Pass.
May I govern, &c.

XVII

With a Courage undaunted, may I face my last
   Day,
And when I am Dead, may the better sort say,
In the Morning, when sober, in the Evening,
   when mellow,
He's gone, and left not behind him his Fellow.
May I govern, &c.

XVIII

Without any Noise when I've pass'd o'r the
   Stage,
And decently acted what part Fortune gave,
And put off my Vests in a chearful Old Age,
May a few honest Fellows see me laid in my
   Grave.
May I govern, &c.

XIX

I care not whether under a Turf, or a Stone,
With any inscription upon it, or none,
If a Thousand Years hence, *Here lies W.P.*,
Shall be read on my Tomb, what is it to me?
May I govern, &c.

XX

Yet one Wish I add, for the sake of those Few
Who in reading these lines any Pleasure shall
    take,
May I leave a good Fame, and a sweet smelling
    Name,
AMEN. Here an End to my WISHES I make.

Chorus

May I govern my Passion with an absolute Sway,
And grow Wiser, and Better, as my Strength
    wears away,
Without Gout, or Stone, by a gentle Decay.

On 21 September 1687 Pope resigned
as Gresham Professor of Astronomy. Seth
Ward died in January 1689 (not 1683 as
Pope says), and in November 1693, when
there was a fire at his lodgings, Pope was
living in Lombard Street in London. He
retired to the country about this time, to
the neighbourhood of Epsom, and occupied
himself with literary pursuits; he had a
paraphrase of the 23rd of Horace's Second
Book of Odes published in *Examen Poeticum*

in 1693, and in the following year he brought out his *Select Novels*, of which six are translated from Cervantes and the seventh, *Patient Grissil*, is translated from Petrarch (whose life he apparently intended to write).[1] The *Life of Seth Ward* followed in 1697, and in 1698 he published *Moral and Political Fables Ancient and Modern. Done into Measurd Prose, intermixd with Ryme*. These are the familiar stories—the Town Mouse and the Country Mouse, The Ant and the Grasshopper, and so on—recounted partly in stanzas and partly in a sort of blank verse; they are not of much merit. The book is dedicated to Chief Justice Holt, and in the dedication Pope refers to himself as having 'been grievously harass'd by a causeless, expensive, litigious, and tedious process'; what this law-suit was is not known. For the last years of his life he was living at Bunhill Fields; he died in 1714, and was buried on 25 June in St. Giles', Cripplegate.

II

Pope's *Life of Seth Ward* was part of a paper battle in which Ward's name and reputation were involved almost by acci-

[1] See note on p. 6 of the 1697 ed. of *The Wish*.

dent. In 1693 there was published *A Specimen of some Errors and Defects in the History of the Reformation of the Church of England; Wrote by Gilbert Burnet, D.D., now Lord Bishop of* Sarum, by 'Anthony Harmer'—actually by Henry Wharton, who had conceived a grudge against Burnet, for, as he believed, having prevented him from being appointed Chaplain to Queen Mary. The book consists of a series of citations from Burnet's *History* with the errors of fact or interpretation meticulously pointed out. Right at the end Wharton excuses himself for not having communicated his corrections directly to the author, as Burnet had asked, by referring to the account given in *Athenae Oxonienses*[1] of Burnet's treatment of William Fulman, whose help had not been properly acknowledged. Burnet seized on this point in his (not very convincing) reply, saying of 'Harmer':

> ... he sends me to a passage in the Second Part of *Athenae Oxonienses*. I confess I did not expect to see a Writer of his *Rank*, descend so low as to cite such a Scribler, especially upon such an occasion. That *poor Writer* has thrown together such a tumultuary mixture of Stuff and Tattle, and has been so visibly a Tool of some of the Church of

[1] Part II (1692), p. 625.

> *Rome*, to Reproach all the greatest Men of
> our Church, that no man who takes care of
> his own Reputation, will take anything upon
> trust that is said by one that has no Reputa-
> tion to lose. . . .[1]

This savours very much of abusing the
plaintiff's attorney, but Burnet goes on,
with rather more justification, to speak of
Wood's having 'barbarously attacked' the
memory of his immediate predecessor, Seth
Ward.[2] Wood in fact, while he pays grudg-
ing tribute to Ward's scientific attainments,
takes several opportunities to refer to his
lack of principle, and especially in Part II
of the *Athenae Oxonienses*, when he is
writing of 'Oxford Bishops'. Here he says
of Ward—and this is the passage to which
Pope refers on p. 20 of his *Life*—that he

> . . . did, about his Majesties Restauration
> 1660 endeavour to make his Loyalty
> known by being imprison'd at *Cambr*, by
> his ejection, his writing against the Cove-
> nant and I know not what, but not a word
> of his cowardly wavering for lucre and
> honour sake, of his putting in and out, and
> occupying other mens places for several
> years, etc.[3]

Wood clearly resented the way in which
the 'virtuosi', apparently without difficulty,

---

[1] *A Letter writ by the Lord Bishop of* Salisbury *to the Lord
Bishop of* Cov. *and* Litchfield . . . 1693: pp. 9–10.
[2] Ibid., p. 10.   [3] *Ath. Oxon.* (1692), II, p. 686.

managed to prosper under the Commonwealth and remain in favour after the Restoration; he makes the same sort of complaint against Wilkins.[1]

Burnet's scathing references were too much for Wood's combative nephew Thomas, fresh from acting as his uncle's Proctor in the suit brought against him in the Vice-Chancellor's court at Oxford for defaming the first Earl of Clarendon, and he replied in *A Vindication of the Historiographer of the University of Oxford and his Work, from the Reproaches of the Lord Bishop of Salisbury, etc.* (1693). Again the bulk of the discussion does not concern Seth Ward; Wood repudiates the charge that his uncle was used by the Catholic party as a tool, discusses Burnet's objections (made in his *History of the Reformation*) against Anthony Wood's account of the role played by Oxford in the matter of Henry VIII's divorce, and so on. He also, however, points out that Burnet had used Wharton's reference to *Athenae Oxonienses* as a red-herring to distract attention from the charges made against his own scholarship, using a striking image to describe Burnet's tactics:

[1] Ibid., p. 371.

I cannot but reflect on that sort of Crea-
ture, who when for their Snarling and Barking, a Stone or a Stick is thrown at them,
they turn Tail to him that threw it, and fall
with Teeth, and Grins upon the poor Instrument of Correction. With Reverence be it
spoken, there is a great likeness in the
present case,[1]

and then goes on to discuss Ward's character, obviously drawing his inspiration from
his uncle:

Had his Lordship known Dr. *Ward*
before His Majesties Restauration, he would
have been of another Mind; but his know-
ledg of him, was not, I presume, till after he
was a Bishop, when then, and to the time of
his Death, he was esteemd a Good and
Excellent Man. The Truth is, he was a
Man of Parts, and a great Royalist for a
Time; but when he saw that King *Charles*
the First was beheaded, and Monarchy never
in a possibility of returning again, then did
he change his Orthodox Principles, submit
to the Men then in power, and Eat the
Bread of Two Royalists (that had been
Ejected,) successively. . . .

What his Life and Conversation was,
while he Lived in *Oxon*, the poor Remnant
of the Royalists that then remained there,
would have told you, who usually said, *That
had not Dr.* Ward *degenerated from their
Principles of Loyalty, he would not have lashed*

[1] P. 25.

out into several Immoralities, &c. for the doing
of which, he also lost the Opinion that the
then Saints in the University had of him.[1]

This passage also was clearly in Pope's mind
when he wrote his defence of his friend.

It might well be doubted whether Pope
was the best man to write a defence of
Ward. Indeed, it might be doubted whether Ward could really be successfully
defended at all. Older than Pope (he was in
fact born in 1617, and not 1618, as Pope
says[2]), Ward was established as Fellow of
Sidney Sussex and University Lecturer in
Mathematics at Cambridge when the Puri-
tans commenced their reformation of the
University in 1644. He certainly suffered
for his principles then, and as Pope says,
was ejected from his posts and forced into
retirement. Pope is careful to point out that
he only accepted the position of Professor of
Astronomy at Oxford at the express request
of the ejected Professor, Greaves, so that he
was not 'eating the Bread of a Royalist', and
this may well be true. Much of the argument, however, hinged on whether Ward
did or did not sign the 'Engagement' to be

[1] Pp. 26–7.
[2] Ward apparently liked to claim that he was born in the
year of the great Comet; see Aubrey's *Brief Lives*, ed. Powell,
p. 175.

faithful to the Commonwealth of England as established without a King or House of Lords. Pope says that Ward was able to take office without submitting, while Wood maintained that he did submit, and that a record of his submission appeared in the Register of the Visitors.[1] This is not so. Nevertheless Ward must have found it difficult to avoid taking the Engagement, for on 6 February 1650 the Visitors directed, in pursuance of an Order of the Committee of Parliament for regulating the University, that the Fellows, Graduates and all Officers of Wadham should appear in Hall the following day and there subscribe to the Engagement, and there is no record of any abstentions.[2] In any case Ward's general conduct was hard to defend. Whether or not he was guilty of 'immorality' while in Oxford, he certainly used his influence on the Puritan side, though very probably, like Wilkins, he was a moderate and tried to avoid excess. Equally certainly, as Bishop of Salisbury he was a notorious persecutor of Nonconformists.[3] Burnet's considered judgment of him is probably a fair one:

[1] *A Vindication*, etc., p. 7; *Appendix to the Life of Seth Ward*, p. 8.   [2] The original Order is in the college archives.
[3] See the references given by Mayor in N & Q (IInd Series), VII, 269.

He was a man of a great reach, went deep in mathematical studies, and was a very dexterous man, if not too dexterous; for his sincerity was much questioned. He was a profound statesman, but a very indifferent clergyman.[1]

Pope tries to distract attention from the tender points of Ward's life by interpolating the account of the Controversy concerning Caps and Hoods when he is dealing with Ward's career at Oxford, and expanding his account of Ward as Bishop of Salisbury by relating the lives of his friends; in fact there is a great deal more art in Pope's digressions than may at first sight appear. On the other hand, there is really no excuse for the interpolation of Turberville's life, or for the insertion of the chapter of critical observations on Ovid. Thomas Wood, who returned to the attack with *An Appendix to the Life of the Right Revd. Father in God SETH Lord Bishop of* Salisbury ... *In a letter to the Author*[2] fastens on these irrelevancies, describing the *Life* as 'a *mixture* of Vanity, gossipping and Quibling Folly',[3]

... drest up in a Comical and Bantering Stile, full of dry Scraps of Latin, Puns, Proverbs, sensless Digressions, long tedious unedifying Tales. . . .[4]

---

[1] *History of his own Time*, ed. Airy. I, pp. 342–3.
[2] 1697. Sometimes found bound together with Pope's *Life*.
[3] P. 5.   [4] Ibid., p. 4.

and accuses Pope of borrowing the 'Method, Transitions, and the Arguments of (his) chapters' from *Don Quixote*.[1] He also alludes darkly to a 'character' of Pope, written by Anthony à Wood and now in the hands of his trustees; this is the passage, eventually printed in 1721, which accuses Pope of leading 'an epicurean and heathenish Life, much like to that of John Donn the Son'.[2] If Pope had seen this, he would have had a much better reason for a personal quarrel than the obviously accidental omission of his name from the list of Proctors in *Athenae Oxonienses*.

However assiduously Pope may have applied himself to his astronomical studies, it is impossible not to feel that he was a dilettante. His *Life of Ward* is very much wanting if it is to be regarded as an 'official' account, for there is only brief mention of Ward's scientific attainments, which were considerable, and a bare reference to his great controversy with Hobbes in 1654–6.

---

[1] Ibid., pp. 6–7. The rest of Wood's *Appendix* is concerned with a legalistic argument as to whether libel of a dead man is possible—harking back to the suit brought against Anthony à Wood by Clarendon's son; in the copy in the Bodleian (80 Rawl. 710) there is a manuscript continuation of the argument, said by Hearne, to whom this copy belonged, to be in the hand of Arthur Charlett.

[2] *Ath. Oxon.*, 1721, II, p. 1095.

Pope seems by temperament to have belonged to the school of Burton rather than that of Bacon, and to have been as much interested in literature as in science. He was a good linguist—besides being a fair Latin scholar[1] he knew French, Italian, Spanish, and Dutch—and appears quite unable to refrain from displaying his knowledge in a parade of facetious scholarship. His presence in the roll of the 'natural philosophers' of the seventeenth century seems almost fortuitous. Perhaps this is unjust, for the concept of the 'many-sided man' was certainly not dead in his day, and many of the early members of the Royal Society were little more than gentlemen of culture interested, among other things, in scientific curiosities. What is beyond dispute is that Pope was a natural-born writer with an unforcedly engaging literary personality, and whatever his *Life of Ward* may lack, it goes a long way towards justifying the title sometimes accorded him of 'the Boswell of the 17th Century'.

[1] There are a number of errors in the Latin passages in the *Life of Ward* (and in the few Greek tags), but some of these may be due to the printer; the original edition seems to have been carelessly proof-read. These errors have been left uncorrected in this reprint, but obvious misprints in the English text have been silently emended.

THE
LIFE

OF THE

Right Reverend Father in God

SETH,

Lord Bishop of Salisbury,

And CHANCELLOR of the

Most Noble Order of the GARTER.

With a brief Account of

Bishop *Wilkins*,	Dr. *Isaac Barrow*,
Mr. *Lawrence Rooke*,	Dr. *Turbervile*,

And others.

Written by Dr. WALTER POPE, Fellow
of the *ROYAL SOCIETY*.

———— ——— —— *Quid foret Iliæ,
Mavortisque Gener, si Taciturnitas,
Obstaret meritis Invida Romuli?* Hor.

LONDON: Printed for *William Keblewhite*,
at the *Swan* in St. *Paul*'s Church-yard. 1697.

To the Honourable

Colonel JOHN WYNDHAM,

of *DORSETSHIRE*

SIR,

I Might easily bring into the Field, and
Muster, a Brigade, if not an Army
of Motives, which compelld me to Dedicate
this Book to you; but because I know you
love Brevity, I shall content my self to
declare to the World only one of them, viz.

Amongst the few Friends I have, for
Old Men generally out-live their Friends,
I could not pitch upon any Patron so fit
as your Self.

For you were intimately acquainted with
the deceased Bishop, the Subject of this
Treatise, lovd him, and was intirely belovd
by him.

I

DEDICATION.

I appeal therefore to you, as Competent Judge, and an Eye-witness, whether what I have said concerning his Hospitality, his humble and obliging Conversation in Salisbury, *be not rather less, than more than it deservd.*

You also, as I find by Experience, bear no small Affection to me, which I humbly beg you to continue, as long as I shall approve my Self,

SIR,

Your most humble, obliged,

and Grateful Servant,

Walter Pope.

THE

THE
LIFE

OF THE

Right Reverend Father in God

SETH,

Lord Bishop of *Salisbury*, *&c.*

CHAP. I. *The Introduction.*

THE Motives that incouraged me, to write this ensuing Treatise, were such as these, *viz.*

1. The deceas'd Bishop had conferred many Favours upon me, and I thought this was a fit opportunity to publish my Gratitude, for them.

2. That

2. That his Life was worthy to be transmitted to Posterity; and that it would be more acceptable to the Learned, that it should be done by me, as well as I could, than not at all; for I have not yet heard of any person who has designed, or attempted it, tho there are more than eight years past, since he died.

3. I am not altogether unprovided for such a Work, having, during my long Acquaintance with Him, and his Friends, inform'd my self, of most of the considerable Circumstances of his Life.

4. And in the fourth and last place, because I shall run no risque in so doing: for tho some may blame my Performance, yet, even they, cannot but approve my pious Intention; and the worst that can be said against me, if I do not attain my end, will have more of Praise, in it, than Reproach, 'tis what *Ovid* says of *Faeton*, *Magnis tamen excidit aufis*, i. e. *'Twas a noble Attempt, but the Success was not answerable.*

I at first design'd to have written it in a continual Narration, without breaking it into Chapters, making any Reflections, or adding any Digressions; but upon second thoughts, which usually are the best, I

steer'd

steer'd another Course, I have cut it into Chapters, which may serve, as Benches in a long Walk, whereupon the weary Reader may repose himself, till he has recovered Breath, and then readily proceed in his way. I have also interwoven some Digressions, which, if they are not too frequent, forein, impertinent, and dull, will afford some Divertisement to the Reader. But I fear the Gate is too great for this little City.

C H A P. II.

Of the Bishops Parentage, Birth, and Education, till he was sent to Cambridge.

I Think it not worth my pains, to play the Herald, and blazon the Arms belonging to the numerous Family of the WARDS, or to tell the World the Antiquity of it; that that Name came into *England* with *William* the Conqueror; that there is at present one Lord, and very many Knights and Gentlemen of very considerable Estates who are so called: For sup-

posing

posing this to be true, as it is, it makes little, if any thing, to the Praise of the Person whose Life I am now writing. *Vix ea nostra voco.* Vertuous Actions, not great Names, are the best Ensigns of Nobility. There are now, always were, and ever will be, some bad Men, even of the best Families, I shall therefore go no further back than to his Grandfather, who lived near *Ipswich* in *Suffolk*, and had the misfortune to lose a considerable hereditary Estate; whereupon the Bishops Father, whose Name was *John*, settled himself at *Buntingford* in *Hertfordshire*, following the Employment of an Attorney, and was of good Reputation, for his fair Practice, but not rich. His Mothers Maiden Name was *Dalton*; I have often heard him commend her extraordinarily, for her Vertue, Piety, and Wisdom, to whose good Instructions and Counsels, he used to say, he ow'd whatever was good in him. And that this Character was due to her, I have the testimony of that worthy Gentleman, *Ralph Freeman* Esq;, of *Aspenden* in *Hertfordshire*, who has faithfully served his Country, as Knight of the Shire for that County in several Parliaments; this Mr. *Freeman* liv'd in the same

Parish,

Parish, and well remembers the Bishops Mother. I never heard the Bishop speak of his Father, possibly he died before his Son came to years of Discretion; on the contrary, I find *Horace* never mentions his Mother, but is very frequently praising his Father; but to proceed.

John Ward left three Sons, and as many Daughters, the Sons were *John*, *Seth*, and *Clement*, *John* died a Batchelour, *Clement* left three Sons, and several Daughters, to the Care of his Brother *Seth*, who had then no other Preferment or Income, than the Place of the *Savilian* Professor of Astronomy in *Oxford*, and even then, he gave two hundred pounds to one of his Sisters in Marriage, which Summ he borrowed of a Friend of his, whom I knew, who lent it him upon his own Bond, without any other Security, μηδὲν ἀνελπιζόμενος, which let me thus translate, since 'tis not *è Cathedra*, *nothing doubting*, or *not despairing to be repaid*, as he was, in a short time, with Thanks and Interest. This Friend of his perceived evident signs of a rising Man in Mr. *Ward*, which must infallibly advance him, if Merit alone can elevate, as it has often, without Friends, under some Kings, and

and some Archbishops: and it will certainly, at long run, if, as the Saying is, *The Horse does not die, before the Grass is grown.*

For all these Male and Female Children, and Relations before mentioned, he provided more than a competent Maintenance, binding some of them Apprentices, breeding others at Schools and Universities, till they were fit for the Ministry, and then placed them in good Benefices, whereof he had the Presentation. He also took care of his Nieces, and provided them Husbands, or to speak more truly, they married themselves to deserving Men, and he preferred their Husbands. I remember he once shew'd me a Letter, he had lately received from a Sister of his, who was a Dissenter, which began thus, *Brother*, for she would not call a Bishop Lord, *Since there is Corn in Egypt, it is not meet that the Children of Israel should want.* I cannot say that this Address prevailed with him, but I am sure it did not hinder him, from filling her Sack. I will anticipate no more of the Bishops Life, but henceforwards proceed methodically.

He was born at *Buntingford*, in the year of our Lord 1618, famous for the appearing

ing and long duration of a great Comet, which some will have to prognosticate the *German* Wars, which happened not long after; but I may as truly say, it foreboded the Greatness of this Man, and I do as much believe the one as the other, that is, not at all.

His good Mother, whom we have mentioned in the beginning of this Chapter, taught him her self, till he was fit for the Grammar School, bending the young Twig to Vertue, and inculcating to him all things that were good and praise-worthy, wherewith he was so well imbued, that he lost not the Savour of her Education till his death. I have often heard him say, that the Precepts which his Mother gave him both Moral and Political, were not inferiour to those which he afterwards found in the best Filosofers.

He had his first rudiments of Latin in the Grammar School at *Buntingford*, tho not the benefit of an happy Institution, his Master being a weak Man; yet by the encouragement of his Mother, and his own Industry and Parts, he made such improvement, that, by competent Judges, he was esteemed fit for the University, at the age of fourteen years, and accordingly he was
sent

sent to *Cambridge*, and admitted into *Sidney* College, *Anno Dom.* 1632.

He was recommended to Doctor *Samuel Ward*, the Master of that College, by Mr. *Alexander Strange*, Vicar of *Buntingford*, a Person of great Integrity and Piety, by whose care and solicitation, the Chapel and School-house of that place were erected. This Dr. *Samuel Ward* was a Person of that eminency for Piety and Learning, that King *James* I. made choice of him amongst others, to assist at the Synod of *Dort*, and a great Friend to Mr. *Strange*, upon whose Recommendation, he took young *Seth* into his more especial care, lodging him in his own Apartment, and allowing him the use of the Library; in a word, treating him, as if he had been his own, and onely Son.

CHAP. III.

Of his being at Cambridge.

WHEN he first went to the University, he was young and low of stature, and as he walked about the streets, the Doctors, and other grave Men, would

frequently

frequently lay their Hands upon his white Head, for he had very fair Hair, and ask him of what College he was, and of what standing, and such like Questions, which was so great a vexation to him, that he was asham'd to go into the Town, and, as it were, forc'd to stay in the College and study. I said before, that he had the benefit of the College Library, and our young Student shew'd this Favour was not ill bestow'd upon him, by making good use of it, and so happily improving that advantage, that in a short time he was taken notice of, not only in that College, but also in the University, as a Youth of great Hopes and Learning, beyond what was usual in one of his age, and standing.

All his Improvement was the product of his happy Genius and Love to Learning, and not due to any Instructions he received either from his School-master or Tutor, for Mr. *Pendrith* his Tutor, tho he was a very honest Man, yet he was no Conjurer, nor of any fame for Learning. I have often heard the Bishop repeat some part of his Tutors Speeches, which never fail'd to make the Auditory laugh.

To omit his other Studies, for there
were

were no Regions of Learning which he had
not visited, I think it not improper here
to relate, that his Genius led him to those
which are above vulgar Capacities, and re-
quire a good Head, and great Application
of Mind to understand.

In the College Library he found, by
chance, some Books that treated of the
Mathematics, and they being wholly new
to him, he inquired all the College over for
a Guide to instruct him that way, but all
Search was in vain, these Books were
Greek, I mean unintelligible, to all the Fellows of the College. Nevertheless, he
took courage, and attempted them himself, *proprio Marte*, without any Confede-
rates, or Assistance, or Intelligence in that
Countrey, and that with so good Success,
that in a short time he not only discovered
those *Indies*, but conquer'd several Kingdoms therein, and brought thence a great
part of their Treasure, which he shew'd
publicly to the whole University not long
after. When he was Sofister, he dispu-
ted in those Sciences, more like a Master
than a Learner, which Disputation Dr. *Bambridge* heard, greatly esteemed, and commended. This was the same Dr. *Bambridge*
who

who was afterwards *Savilian* Professor of Astronomy at *Oxford*, a learned and good Mathematician; yet there goes a Story of him, which was in many Scholars Mouths when I was first admitted there, That he put upon the School Gate an *Affiche*, or written Paper, as the Custom is, giving notice, at what time, and upon what Subject the Professor will read, which ended in these Words, *Lecturus de Polis & Axis*, under which was written by an unknown Hand, as follows,

Doctor *Bambridge*, came from *Cambridge*,
    To read *De Polis & Axis*.   (came,
Let him go back again, like a Dunce as he
    And learn a new *Syntaxis*.

But this by the by, let us return to our Charge, at his Act for Batchelour of Arts, his Questions were concerning the *Julian* and *Gregorian* Account of the Year, which gave occasion to Mr. *Thorndike*, then Proctor, to take especial notice of him, and intitled him to the Acquaintance and Friendship of most of his ingenious Contemporaries, amongst whom, some prov'd afterwards very eminent, as Dr. *Pearson*, the learned Bishop

Bishop of *Chester*, Sir *Charles Scarborough*,
Mr.*Rook*,*&c.* Of some of them, I shall have
occasion to speak elsewhere.

In the year 1640. Dr. *Cousins* was Vice-
chancellour, and he pitcht upon Mr. *Ward*
to be *Prævaricator*, which in *Oxford* we call
Terræ-filius, and in that place he behaved
himself to the general Satisfaction of the
Auditory; but yet, it must be acknowledged, that the Vice-chancellour took
some offence at his Speech, and suspended
him his Degree.

Dr. *Cousins* was not an Enemy to Wit,
but perhaps he thought not fit to allow it
to be so freely spoken, in so sacred a Place.
I say he took some offence against him, but
whether 'twas given or only taken, I determine not, but however the next day
before the end of the *Commencement*, for
what at *Oxford* is called the *Act*, is stiled
by that Name at *Cambridge*, he revers'd his
Censure. The Reader may imagine his
Fault was not great, when so severe a
Judge, as Bishop *Cousins*, should impose no
greater Punishment upon him, and take it
off in so short a time. I had not mention'd
this his Suspension, neither ought I, had it
not, many years after, made a great noise at
Oxford,

Oxford, which we shall mention in its proper place. Both Dr. *Cousins*, and Mr. *Ward*, were not long after, Fellow Sufferers in another and far greater Cause; and he certainly suffer'd without any Fault then, whatever he did before.

The Civil Wars breaking out, the Effects of them were first felt by the Bishops, and afterwards by the Universities: *Cambridge* suffer'd first, lying in the associated Counties, and subject to the Parliaments Power; *Oxford*, which was then a Garrison, and the Kings Head-quarters, drank of the same bitter Cup some years after. At *Cambridge*, several Heads and Fellows of Colleges and Halls were imprisoned, for refusing the Covenant, some in the Town, and some in St. *Johns* College, made a Gaol by the Parliament Forces, commanded by the Earl of *Manchester*; and amongst the rest Dr. *Samuel Ward*, Master of *Sidney* College was imprisoned, whither Mr. *Ward* accompanied him voluntarily, and submitted to that Confinement, that he might assist so good a Man, and so great a Friend in that Extremity. I have heard him say, that Imprisonment seem'd at first to him

very

very uneasie, but after he had been a little time used to it, he liked it well enouf, and could have been contented, not to have stir'd out all the days of his Life. The great Inconvenience of so close a Confinement, in the heighth of a hot Summer, caused some of Doctor *Wards* Friends to mediate for his Removal, at least for some Weeks, which was granted, and in the beginning of *August*, the Doctor was permitted to go to his own House, to which also Mr. *Ward* accompanied him, and carefully ministred unto him. Within a Months time after his Inlargement, the good old Man fell into a dangerous Distemper, caused by his Imprisonment, whereof he died the seventh of *September* following, in the year of our Lord 1643. Mr. *Ward*, who never left him, was with him in the last moments of his Life, and closed his Eyes, after having received his last Words, which were these, *God bless the King, and my Lord Hopton,* who then commanded a great Army in the West. What befel him afterwards, during his stay at *Cambridge*, shall be the Subject of the next Chapter.

CHAP.

CHAP. IV.

A Continuation of the Precedent Matter.

UPON the Death of Dr. *Ward*, the Fellows assembled to chuse a new Master. Mr. *Ward*, with nine of them, gave their Suffrages for Mr. *Thorndike* of *Trinity* College; for Mr. *Minshull* there were eight votes, including his own, but while they were at the Election, a Band of Soldiers rusht in upon them, and forcibly carried away Mr. *Parsons*, one of those Fellows who voted for Mr. *Thorndike*, so that the number of Suffrages for Mr. *Mynshull*, his own being accounted for one, was equal to those Mr. *Thorndike* had. Upon which Mr. *Mynshull* was admitted Master, the other eight only protesting against it, being ill advised, for they should have adher'd to their Votes. Two of them, whereof Mr. *Ward* was one, went to *Oxford*, and brought thence a *Mandamus* from the King, commanding Mr. *Mynshull* and the Fellows of *Sidney* College, to repair thither, and give an account of their Proceedings, as to
that

that Election, this *Mandamus* or peremtory
Summons was fix'd upon the Chapel door,
by Mr. *Linnet*, who was afterwards a Fellow of *Trinity* College, but at that time attended on Mr. *Thorndike*. On the other
side, one Mr. *Bertie*, a Kinsman of the Earl
of *Lindsey*, being one of those who voted for Mr. *Mynshull*, was also sent to *Oxford* in his behalf; this Gentleman, by the
Assistance and Mediation of my Lord of
Lindsey, procur'd an Order from the King,
to confirm Mr. *Mynshulls* Election, but he,
not thinking this Title sufficient, did corroborate it with the Broad Seal, to which
Mr. *Thorndike* consented, Mr. *Mynshull* pay-
ing him and the rest of the Fellows the
Charges they had been at, in the Management of that Affair, amounting to about an
hundred pound. The next Spring Mr. *Ward*
and Mr. *Gibson* were summoned to appear
before the Committee of Visitors, then sitting at *Trinity* College, and tender'd the
Covenant, and other Oaths, which they
refused, declaring themselves unsatisfied as
to the Lawfulness of them. Then they desired to know if the Committee had any
Crime to object against them? they answe-
red they had not; they declared the reason
why

why they ask'd was, that they understood,
some were ejected for not taking the Covenant, and others for Immoralities; to
which they received this Answer, that those
were words of course, put into all their Orders of Ejection. Such was the Carriage
of those Commissioners, not only to take
away the Livelyhood of those they expell'd,
but also their good Name and Reputation,
and so render them unpitied, and not worthy to be relieved.

In the Month of *August* following, Mr.
Ward, who was then absent, received the
news, that his Ejection was voted and put
into Execution.

Being now exil'd from *Cambridge*, he di-
verted himself with Dr. *Wards* Relations,
in and about *London*, for a season, and
sometimes with the Reverend Divine and
Learned Mathematician, Mr. *William Oughtred*, invited thereto by his Love to those
Sciences, in which Mr. *Oughtred* had shew'd
his Ability, and acquir'd a great Name by
publishing his *Clavis Mathematicæ*, a little
Book as to the bulk, but a great one as to
the Contents, as the understanding Reader
must acknowledge.

Mr. *Ward* was so well known, and of so
good

good a reputation at *Cambridge*, that in his Exile he wanted not places of resort and refuge. He was invited by the E. of *Carlile*, and several other Persons of high Quality, with proffers of large and honourable Pensions, to come and reside in their Families: Nay, I have heard him say, that even then when he was in those straights, and might have truly said, Silver, or Gold, or Preferment I have none, he was proffer'd several rich Matches, but he had no inclination to Matrimony, whilst he labour'd under those Circumstances. At last he chose to accept the Invitation, or to speak more properly, to yield to the importunity of his Friend and Country-man *Ralf Freeman* Esquire, of *Aspenden* in *Hertfordshire*, in the Parish wherein he suck'd his first Milk, and imbib'd his first rudiments of Vertue, about five and twenty mile distant from *London*; he instructed his Sons, and continued there off and on, till the Year 1649. Then he was earnestly invited by my Lord *Wenman* of *Tame-Park* in *Oxfordshire*, about ten miles distant from that City, thither he went, and liv'd some time with him, rather as a Companion than Chaplain, it being more safe for him to be near *Oxford* than *Cambridge*, and

as

as it prov'd in the event, much more advantageous, for this was the first visible step to his preferment. He was not in this Family many months before the Visitation of the University of *Oxford* began; the Effect whereof was, that many Heads of Colleges and Halls, as also many Fellows of Colleges were turn'd out, as before at *Cambridge*, and at last the Visitation reach'd the learn'd and eminent Person Mr. *Edw. Greaves*, *Savilian* Professor of Astronomy, and Fellow of *Merton-College*, the same who had but a little before publish'd that learned Exercitation concerning the Measuring of the fam'd *Egyptian* Pyramides near *Grand Cairo*.

Altho' this Gentleman was for a season skreen'd against the fury of the Visitation by some powerful Friends, yet finding that 'twas impossible for him to keep his ground, he made it his business to procure an able and worthy Person to succeed him. Upon that design he took a Journey to *London*, to advise with some knowing Persons concerning that Affair; and amongst the rest with Dr. *Scarborough*, who had then very great Practice, and liv'd magnificently, his Table being always accessible to all learned Men,

Men, but more particularly to the distressed Royalists, and yet more particularly to the Scholars ejected out of either of the Universities for adhering to the Kings Cause. After mature Consultation, it was agreed upon by a general consent, that no Person was so proper and fit for that employment as Mr. *Ward*. Mr. *Greaves*, who had heard much of Mr. *Ward*, but had no acquaintance with him, readily consented to what they had concerted, and undertook to find Mr. *Ward* out, and make him the proffer, and accordingly he made a Journey to *Oxford*. Mr. *Ward* wholly ignorant of this design upon him, or rather for him, rides casually from *Tame-Park* to *Oxford*, as he frequently us'd to do, either to consult some Books in the public Library, or to visit his Friends and Acquaintance. Just as he was entring the *Bear*-Inn, luckily meets Mr. *Greaves* coming out of it, who being inform'd who he was, accosted and courteously saluted him, testifying his great joy by many kind Expressions, for this fortunate and unexpected rencounter; after which, taking him aside, he imparted his business, the design he had to have him for his Successor, urging him with great importunity, not to deny

deny him this favour. I remember I have heard the Bishop say, that amongst other Arguments, Mr. *Greaves* told him, if you refuse it, they will give it to some Cobler of their Party who never heard the name of *Euclid*, or the Mathematics, and yet will greedily snap at it for the Salaries sake. But Mr. *Greaves* was out in his Divination, for the other Place, I mean the Professors of Geometry, was fill'd with a very learned Man in that Science, as his elaborate Works have sufficiently manifested to the World. This Address of Mr. *Greaves* did so surprize Mr. *Ward*, that it did at once assault his Modesty, and perplex his Council. After many thanks for so great and unexpected a Favour, he objected the difficulty of effecting it, saying, he could not with any reason expect, to enjoy quietly a public Professors place in *Oxford*, when 'twas notoriously known, that he was turn'd out of *Cambridge* for refusing the Covenant. Mr. *Greaves* reply'd, that he and his Friends had consider'd that Obstacle, and found out a way to remove it, and it was effectually remov'd a little while after by the means of Sir *John Trevor*, who tho' of the Parliament Party, was a great lover of Learning, and

and very obliging to several Scholars who had been turn'd out of the two Universities. Sir *John* had great Interest in the Committee which dispos'd of the Places of those who were ejected, and by that brought Mr. *Ward* into the Professors Chair, and preserv'd him in it, without taking the Covenant, or Engagement. So that the very same thing that caus'd his ejection out of *Cambridge*, was the cause also of his preferment in *Oxford*. The first Astronomy Professor, I mean of Sir *Henry Saviles* Foundation, was a *Cambridge* Man, plac'd in by the Founder, as was also the Geometry Professor put in now by the Visitors, the difference of Universities being not esteem'd a sufficient obstacle to hinder any deserving Persons from obtaining either of these Places. Mr. *Ward* being now settled in the Professors Chair, was in the first place careful to express his Gratitude to those Persons, by whose assistance he had obtain'd it; and first to Mr. *Greaves*, for whom he procur'd the full Arrears of his Salary, amounting to five hundred pound, for part, if not all the Land allotted to pay the *Savilian* Professors lies in *Kent*, which County was in the power of the Parliament, who with-held the Money, and

and it had been difficult, if not impossible, for Mr. *Greaves*, who was not *Rectus in Curia*, ever to have recover'd it; and he also design'd him a considerable part of his Salary, but he, I mean Mr. *Greaves*, died soon after. To Sir *John Trevor*, Father of that Sir *John*, who was afterwards Secretary of State in the Reign of King *Charles* the Second, he dedicated one of his Books, and therein publicly declares to the World, how many and great Obligations he had to that worthy Person. How Mr. *Ward* behav'd himself at *Oxford*, and what befel him there, will be the Subject of the ensuing Chapters.

CHAP. V.

Of his being at Oxford.

AND now I have brought him to *Oxford*, where I first became acquainted with him, I can proceed upon more certain grounds; I promise not to put any thing upon the Reader now, but what either I knew, or have heard attested by those whom I could trust. Hitherto I have been guided, for the greatest part, by what I have

have recived from the Bishop himself, casually, and at several times. I am also indebted, for the Names of the Bishops Relations, to that worthy Person *Ralf Freeman* Esquire, whom I have had occasion so often to mention before, and shall again; one whom he lov'd and honour'd all his Life, and to whom, and his Heirs, he left, at his Death, the sole power of putting in his Alms-men, as will be related in its due place.

The greatest Light concerning the *Cambridge* Transactions before related, I received by a few short indigested Notes, which Dr. *Sherman* had collected, in order to write the Bishops Life, this Dr. *John Sherman*, was the Bishop of *Salisburys* Chaplain, and Arch-deacon of North *Wiltshire*, a very learned Person, and would, had he out-liv'd the Bishop, been the fittest Man in the World to have undertaken the Task, which I, for want of others, am engaged in. But he was untimely cut off by the Small Pox, at the Bishop of *Salisburys* Lodgings in *Charterhouse-yard*, *March* 24. *Anno Dom.* 1671. many years before the Bishop, whose Life he had designed to have writtten.

The first thing Mr. *Ward* did, after his

Settlement

Settlement in *Oxford*, was to bring the A-
stronomy Lectures into Reputation, which
had been for a considerable time disused,
and wholly left of. He therefore read very constantly, and, that being known, he
never fail'd of a good Auditory; I have
heard him say, and he was no Lyar, that
in all the time he enjoy'd the Astronomy
Professors Place, he never miss'd one reading Day. Besides this, he taught the Mathematics *gratis* to as many of the University,
or Foreigners, as desired that Favour of
him. I remember he told me that a certain *German* Nobleman made application to
him upon that account, and that when
Mr. *Ward* was in the middle of a hard
Demonstration, which required the utmost
Intention of Mind to understand, for if
by Inadvertency, one Link of it is lost,
all the rest is to no purpose and unintelligible; this Person interrupted him and said
Sir you have a fine Key, his Key by chance
lying then upon the Table; 'tis so, reply'd the Professor, and put an End to his
Lecture, and would read no more to that
Pupil.

Besides this, he preach'd frequently,
tho' he was not obliged to it, for Sir *Henry*
Savile

Savile had exempted his Professors from all University Exercises, that they might have the more leisure to mind the Employment he designed them for. His Sermons were strong, methodical and clear, and, when Occasion required, pathetical and eloquent: for, besides his Skill in the Mathematics, he was a great Lover of *Tully*, and understood him very well. In his Disputations his Arguments were always to the purpose, and managed with great Art, his Answers clear and full. I remember I heard him oppose, in the Act time, a Head of a House, who then did his Exercise for Doctor in Divinity, the Question was, concerning the Morality of the Fourth Commandment, against which he urged, " That the " same time might be *Saturday*, *Sunday* and " *Monday*, or *Sunday* and any two other " days equally distant from it: for suppo- " sing two Ships to set sail from the same " Port, one westward, according to the " Motion of the Sun, it will make every day " longer than four and twenty Hours, and " consequently there must be fewer days in " that Year; and the other, which we sup- " pose holds its course Eastward, must have " the contrary Effect, and consequently
" make

" make more days in the same space of
" time. Let us then suppose that these
" two Ships sail'd at the same time from
" the same place, and return thither that
" day twelve-month, it shall be to one of
" them *Monday*, and to the other *Saturday*.
" Or, supposing two Swallows, with grea-
" ter Celerity, to make the same Voyage,
" both of them starting upon the same *Sun-*
" *day* from the same place, and granting
" one of them to gain, and the other lose,
" about half a quarter of an hour, or eight
" minutes in four and twenty hours which
" they may do, at their Return to the
" place from whence they set forth, tho
" 'twill be *Sunday* to those who remained
" there, it shall be to one of these Swal-
" lows *Tuesday*, and to the other *Friday*.
" Again, if the *Sabbath* is to be accounted
" from Sun-set to Sun-set, as some observe
" it, then to those who inhabit under the
" Poles, it must be a year long for the Sun
" under the Northern Pole sets only in *Sep-*
" *tember*, at the Autumnal *Equinox*, and to
" those under the Southern Pole it sets only
" in *March* or the Vernal *Equinox*. To those
" who lie more Northward than the *Arctic*
" *Circle*, or more Southward than the *Ant-*
" *arctic*,

E

" *arctic*, the *Sunday* shall not only be seve-
" ral Days, but Weeks and Months long.
And several other Arguments of this Nature: To all which the Respondent vouch-
safed no other Answer than this, *Omnia hu-
jusmodi Argumenta sunt mere Astronomica.*
As much as if he should have said, *These
are all but Demonstrations, and therefore, I
think them not worthy of an Answer.*

Whilst he continued in that Chair, besides his Public Lectures he wrote several
Books, one *De Astronomia Eliptica*, one a-
gainst *Bullialdus*, one about *Proportion*, one
of *Trigonometry*, one against Mr. *Hobbs*,
who never pardoned him for it to his dying Day, as we shall have occasion to shew
hereafter, and one, in *English*, and a jocose
stile, against one *Webster*, asserting the Use-
fulness of the Universities. He also preach'd
often, at St. *Maries*, to the Admiration of
all the Auditory, some of which Sermons
are published in the Collection printed for
James Collins.

At his first coming to *Oxford*, he made
choice of *Wadham* Col. to reside in, invited
thereto by the Fame of Dr. *Wilkins* Warden
thereof, with whom he soon contracted an
intimate Acquaintance and Friendship, their
Humours

Humours and Studies lying the same way;
but Dr. *Wilkins* was so well known, that I
need not dilate in his Praise, for if I should,
my near Relation to him, might make my
Character of him suspected, therefore I shall
say no more of him at present, but that he
was a Learned Man, and a Lover of such;
he was of a Comely Aspect, and Gentle-
man-like Behaviour; he had been bred in
the Court, and was also a piece of a Tra-
veller, having twice seen the Prince of *Au-
ranges* Court, at the *Hague*, in his Journey
to, and Return from *Heydelburgh*, whither
he went to wait upon the Prince Elector
Palatine, whose Chaplain he was in *England*. He had nothing of Bigottry, Unman-
nerliness, or Censoriousness, which then
were in the *Zenith*, amongst some of the
Heads, and Fellows of Colleges in *Oxford*.
For which Reason many Country Gentlemen, of all Persuasions, but especially those
then stiled Cavaliers and Malignants, for
adhering to the King and the Church,
sent their Sons to that College, that they
might be under his Government. I shall
instance but in two eminent Sufferers for
that Cause, Colonel *Penruddoc* who was
murder'd at *Exeter*, and Judge *Jenkyns*,

who

who was kept a close Prisoner till the Kings Return, for not owning the Parliaments usurp'd Authority, these two had their Sons there. I could name many more, who for Dr. *Wards* sake, left *Cambridge*, and brought their Pupils with them, and settled themselves in *Wadham* College, as Dr. *Gaspar Needham*, and Mr. *Lawrence Rooke*, of whom I have much to say in its due place.

The Affluence of Gentlemen was so great, that I may truly say of *Wadham* College, it never since, or before, was in so flourishing a Condition, I mean, it never had so many Fellow Commoners as at that time, tho it cannot be denied, but that it has always had more than its proportion; may it for ever flourish and encrease in Riches and Reputation: this I heartily wish, for the Kindness I have received from it.

At this time there were several Learned Men of the University and in the City, who met often at the Wardens Lodgings in *Wadham* College, and sometimes elsewhere, to improve themselves by making Filosofical Experiments. Some of these, for I will not undertake to reckon them all up, were Mr. *Robert Boyle*, then well known, but since more famous in all parts of *Europe*, for

for his great Piety, and Skill in Experimental Filosofy, and other good Literature; Mr. *Matthew Wren*, afterwards Secretary to the Duke of *York*; Dr. *Willis*, Dr. *Goddard*, Warden of *Merton*, and Professor of Fysic at *Gresham* College in *London*, Dr. *Wallis*, Dr. *Bathurst*, Mr. *Rooke*, &c.

About this time that Learned and Reverend Person Dr. *Brownrig*, the ejected Bishop of *Exeter*, came and lived a retired Life, at *Sunning* in *Berkshire*, whither Mr. *Ward*, who was his Chaplain, us'd to go often to wait upon him. This Bishop sent once for him, and collated on him the Precentorship of the Church of *Exeter*, the Incumbent whereof was lately Dead, and at the same time told him, That he was confident the King would be restored, and you may live, said he, to see that happy day, tho I believe I shall not, and then this, which seems now Δῶρον ἄδορον, may be of some Emolument to you. It fell out as the good Bishop foretold, for he died in the dawn of the Restoration, and Mr. *Ward* lived to enjoy this collated Benefice, which was worth to him several thousand pounds. I have heard him often declare, that had he not been Chanter of *Exeter*, he could not have
lived

lived at the rate he always after did, and done those Deeds of Charity, without immersing himself into so great Debt, that he could never be able to pay, and he hated nothing more, than to lye in any Mans debt. To evidence this, I remember, that afterwards, when he was Bishop of *Salisbury*, he never would go out of the Town, either to *London*, whither his Business often called him, or elsewhere, if he intended to make any stay, before he paid all the Tradesmen, with whom he dealt, the uttermost Farthing.

But to proceed, for this Instrument of his Collation, he paid Bishop *Brownrigs* Secretary the full Fees, as if he were presently to take possession of the Place, tho this happened in the darkest night of Despair, when there appeared no Probability, scarcely any Possibility, that the Sun would ever rise again; I mean, the King, Laws, and Church should ever be restor'd. I know he was sufficiently laught at, by some of his Friends, for so doing, I have heard them tell him, they would not give him half a Crown for his Procentorship, to whom he reply'd, since it was the good Bishops Kindness, tho he should never make

a

a peny of it, it was as acceptable to him, as if he were to take possession the next moment.

This was the first fair Flower that ever grew in his Garden, and the foundation of his future Riches and Preferment.

Anno Domini 1654. both the *Savilian* Professors did their Exercises in order to proceed Doctors in Divinity, and when they were to be presented, the other claim'd to be Senior. Mr. *Ward* demanded what pretence have you for this demand, you can't deny, but that I was your Senior in *Cambridge.* The other urg'd that he was suspended from his Degree, as we have mentioned before in the Second Chapter, not remembring, or at least not calling to mind, that he was restor'd before the End of the Commencement, and completed Master, by the Vice-Chancellors putting on Mr. *Wards* Cap before his. When this pretence fail'd, he had recourse to another, and own'd himself to be possest of an Estate, whose value put him into the number of Grand Compounders, who because they pay greater Fees, have the privilege to be Seniors in all Faculties and Degrees of their Year. Thus he obtain'd the Seniority, and pay'd for it, and enjoy'd it, till Dr. *Ward* was made a Bishop.

Bishop. But since this slight difference bred
no Animosities, or ill blood, betwixt the
two Professors, and they liv'd in mutual
kindness till Bishop *Ward*'s death, I shall
insist no longer upon it.

Tho' he was so complyant and useful in
his Station at *Oxford*, yet he could never
wear off, neither indeed did he desire it,
the imputation of being a Cavalier, and
Episcopaly inclin'd, this was often hit in
his teeth, as the unpardonable Sin, and the
Leaven of the Farisees, but it did him no
hurt. Amongst the rest a Person of Honour,
afterwards married to a Peer of this Realm,
who then lived about twenty miles distant
from *Oxford*, in a Family well known to
Dr. *Wilkins* and Dr. *Ward*, and often visited
by them. This Lady drolling with him,
used these words. *Doctor* Ward, *I am confident you believe the King will come in, and
that you shall be a Bishop. Madam*, replyed
he, *I think neither the one or the other impossible. But I esteem it so improbable*, said
she, *that if it happens in my life-time, I promise, before these Witnesses, to present you
with a pair of Lawn Sleeves of mine own
handiwork, which would be no small Mortification to one of our perswasion*, said she laugh-
ing,

ing, for she was a Presbyterian, and yet, nevertheless, which is remarkable, a very Ingenious Lady. Doctor *Ward* return'd her his humble thanks, adding, *If there should be an occasion, he would give her Ladyship timely notice.* And he was as good as his word, giving her advice of his Nomination to the Bishopric of *Exeter.* She also was not worse than hers, presenting him the first Lawn Sleeves he ever wore; and still, notwithstanding his being a Bishop, kept the same Friendship and acquaintance with her, as before. About this time happened a Controversie in the University of *Oxford* about Formalities, in which I bore a great part, and for varieties sake, would have related here, but because this Chapter is long enouf, I reserve it to the next.

CHAP. VI.

The Controversie concerning Caps *and* Hoods.

IN the Year 1658. the reigning Party in the University of *Oxford*, or if you will stile them by the name they assum'd to themselves, the *Godly Party*, began to put all

all things into Confusion; and to that end, in the first place they resolv'd to take away those decent distinctions of Degrees, Caps, and Hoods, and they had done it by a Law, had not I stood in the Gap. *Meme-nisse juvat*, the remembrance whereof is pleasant, *Sumo superbiam quæsitam meritis*, Let no Man rob me of my deserved Ho-nour. The manner was thus; but before I enter into that Narration, I'll tell you one property of this Party: They continually complained of Persecution; I heard one of them Preach at St. *Marys*, his design was to prove, that Afflictions were the lot of the Righteous; but he made this Objection against his Doctrine; *How is this*, said he, *true of us, can we say, we are afflicted and persecuted? When we have all the good things our hearts can wish, we are the Favourites of the Government, and in possession of the best Places, both in the University and Country. To which*, said he, *thus I answer*; *We are, my beloved, Tongue-persecuted; the Wicked for-bear not to say of us, we are Knaves and Hy-pocrites*, which was too true of a great number of them. But to return to my Re-lation: This Party resolv'd to abolish the Statute, enjoyning the wearing of Caps and

and Hoods, crying out against them as Reliques of Popery, and Rags of the Scarlet Whore. To effect this their design, they sent an Envoy to me to engage me to comply with them, well knowing that without my concurrence their design would prove abortive. The Person whom they employed was a Schoolfellow and intimate Friend of mine, who altho' the Son of a Royalist, upon some disappointments, especially a great one, that happened to him at *Westminster* by the means of Mr. *Busby*, of which perhaps more hereafter: I say, upon this, and other Misfortunes, he became a Presbyterian and Commonwealths-Man, if this addition be not superfluous. He was a Man of Learning, and knew it, and very hot and zealous in his way; he, I say, came to my Chamber and told me his Message. Well, said I to him, what have you to say against Caps and Hoods? He made a long Discourse, which I heard with patience; and when I perceiv'd he was silent, *Ned*, said I to him, prithee go back to thy Chamber, and put in writing all that thou hast said, and bring it to me. And what will you do with it then, said he? I will, I reply'd, blot out the words Caps and Hoods,

and

and in their places insert Gowns; will not your Arguments be every whit as strong against them, as against Formalities? I confess they will, he answer'd, but we are not come thither yet. I replyed, I'd make it my endeavour to keep you where you are, and so we parted.

As I was confident the Party would drive on the design furiously, so I saw that without me they could never bring it to take effect; there being a Statute, which says in express Terms, That no Statute be deem'd abrogated or repeal'd, without the attestation of the Vice-Chancellor, and both the Proctors, under their hands, that it was formally taken away in the Convocation. But before I proceed any further in this Contest, give me leave to make a small digression, and recount what afterwards befel this my Friend. I hinted before a great disappointment he had received from Mr. *Busby* the School-master of *Westminster*, the matter of Fact was thus; Mr. *Vincent* the second Master, left that Station, and went to Travel for his Health, then did Mr. *Busby* write to my Friend, who was Master of Arts, and Student of *Christ-Church*, to come and be Second Master. After he had receiv'd this

Letter,

Letter, brimful of joy, he brought it me, thinking I should, as his Friend, be also much pleas'd at this good News, and encourage him to accept of this proffer: But I, contrary to his expectation, us'd my utmost endeavour to diswade him from it. He answer'd, that I spoke out of prejudice against Mr. *Busby*, but he knew better things. 'Tis true, when he was a Kings Scholar at *Westminster*, he was a little, well-favour'd, white-hair'd Youth, and his Father was liberal to the Master; all which concurring with a good docible Inclination, made him one of Mr. *Busbys* White Boys, or chief Favourites. But I foresaw the Case would soon be alter'd, when he should pretend Equality, and not content himself to keep at such a distance as the former Usher did; I told him, there is a great difference betwixt you and Mr. *Vincent*; he was a very honest and learned Man, but of mean Parentage, Mr. *Busbys* Servitor at *Oxford*, and but one remove from it, at *Westminster*, you are a Gentleman, and of no submissive Temper, you have had liberal Education, and kept good Company, and know the World, 'tis impossible you can submit to such Usage, as you will find there. For I
very

very well knew both their Humours, and easily foresaw, that 'twas absolutely impossible for those two, as the Saying is, to set their Horses together. The event prov'd that I was on the right side of the Hedge, he found such Usage as I foretold, and I doubt not, but his Behaviour was, as I conjectur'd it would be, but the particulars thereof are too long, and not necessary to be here related. Upon this he turns, turns with a vengeance, goes over to the Gentiles, and that he might be reveng'd upon Mr. *Busby*, Sacrifices to *Moloch*, worships, and adores the worst of Men, even the Judges of King *Charles* the First; but Mr. *Busby*, who Plow'd with the same Heifers, had too much complyance, cunning, and money, to be hurt by him. Upon this, he returns to his Students Place at *Christ-Church*, makes me a Visit, and rails so bitterly against Mr. *Busby*, that, even I was forc'd to take his part. He remain'd at *Oxford*, propagating his Commonwealth Principles, and when he was Censor, which Office in other Colleges is call'd the Dean, whose business 'tis, to Moderate at Disputations, and give the Scholars Questions; he gave some in Politics, and

and order'd the Respondents to maintain them against Monarchy and Episcopacy. There he continued till the King was restor'd, then some considerable Friends of his, whom I knew, advis'd him to go into the Country, and there to live peaceably, and conformably, for the space of one Year, at the end of which, they assur'd him, they would procure him some considerable Preferment in the Church. Accordingly he went, and tryed, but not being able to hold out so long, in a short time he repair'd to *London*, seven times more imbitter'd against Ecclesiastical and Kingly Government than when he went into the Country: And now he sides Tooth and Nail with the Fanatics, and made a great Figure amongst them, exceeding most, if not all of them, in Natural and acquir'd parts. King *Charles* sent for him, designing to work some good upon him, and do him a kindness; but he found him so obstinate and refractory, that he was forc'd to leave him to his own Imaginations; he afterwards married a blind Woman, who fell in Love with him for his Preaching; after which I met him in *Covent-Garden*, and accosted him freely; after the usual Complements past, *Ned*, said I to him

him jocularly, I hear thou hast married a blind Woman, dost thou intend to beg with her? Upon this I perceiv'd his Countenance change, and he return'd me this Answer; What's that to you; may not I Marry whom I please? Nay, said I, if you are pleas'd, I have no reason to be offended, and so we parted, and I never saw him after, but I understood since, that he died a Prisoner in a House near *Newgate*, whither he was committed for his violent opposition to the Government. It is now full time I should reassume the Clue of my Narration. The Vice-Chancellor summons a Convocation, having most of the Heads of Houses, and many Masters of Arts on his side. It was very remarkable, that all the Antediluvian Cavaliers, I mean Fellows of Colleges, who had the good fortune to survive the Flood of the Visitation, and keep their Places, and who had ever since that liv'd retir'd in their Cells, never medling with Public Affairs in the University, nor appearing in the Convocation, or Congregations, came now as it were in Troops, *Velut Agmine facto*, habited in their Formalities, to give their Votes for their Continuation, most of whose Faces were unknown to the greatest

part

part of the Assembly; with these unexpected recruits we easily carried our Cause, tho' we could have done it without their Assistance. After the Cause of the Convocation was declar'd, as the Custom is, the Vice-Chancellor put it to the Vote, Whether the Statute commanding the Use of Caps and Hoods, should be abrogated, or not: After the Scrutiny, he declar'd, tho' he knew nothing of the matter, that it was taken away, the other Proctor not resisting or opposing, then I took the boldness to tell the Vice-Chancellor, that the majority of Suffrages was to the contrary, as it was in truth; but if it had not been so, I had a Sheet Anchor in reserve, which I would have cast out, rather than have lost my Ship. That was this; There is a Statute, amongst others to which we were Sworn, that declares their Votes Null who are not in Habits suitable to their degrees; almost all their Party, not knowing, or not minding this, came and Voted without their Habits, and consequently lost their Votes; but I was not forc'd to make use of this last Shift, I told the Vice-Chancellor that the Statutes intrust the Proctors only, to gather and compare the Suffrages, and pronounce where the

Majority

Majority fell, and that, with his favour, he had nothing to do in that Affair; to which he reply'd, *Egregie Procurator tace, Good Mr. Proctor hold your tongue*: Upon this, the Masters, in a tumultuary manner, rose from their Seats, and began to Mutiny, which caus'd the Vice-Chancellor to Dissolve the Convocation. One would have thought this business should have ended here, but it did not, for the very next day the Vice-Chancellor sent one of the Beadles to me, desiring me to come to his Lodgings, and there attest under my hand, that the Statute in debate was legally abrogated in the Convocation held the day before. I was wonderfully amaz'd at this Message, I therefore bid him that brought it, to present my Service to the Vice-Chancellor, and withal, to tell him, that I wonder'd he should esteem me so great a Fool, Knave, or Coward, or all of them together, that I should be prevail'd upon to give it under my hand, that I was Perjur'd, when I had acted according to my Oath, and the Truth; I bid him tell him farther, that I should as soon, nay sooner, cut off my Hand and send it to him, as to do what he requir'd, to which there was no rejoyn-
der,

der, and so this Affair ended. The event whereof was, that they who before car'd not whether they wore Caps or Hoods, or not, now immediately procur'd them; never had the Makers and Sellers thereof a better vent for their Ware, as it appear'd the next *Sunday*, for there was then a greater number of Scholars at St. *Marys* in their Formalities, than ever I saw before or since that time, and the Use of them continued, tho' not to that heighth, till the happy Restoration of King *Charles*, which was in less than two Years after.

CHAP. VII.

What happened to Dr. Ward *at* Oxford.

'TIS the natural effect of Eminency, to create Envy in those who despair to arrive to it; the brighter the Sun shines upon any body, the darker is the Shadow, which is inseparable from it. 'Twas well said of *Cleaveland*, '*Tis Heighth makes* Grantham *Steeple stand awry*. Upon this account, Dr. *Ward*, as well as Dr. *Wilkins*, became liable to the Persecutions of those peevish People, who

who ceas'd not to Clamour, and even to Article against them, as *Cavaliers in their hearts, meer Moral Men, without the Power of Godliness*; for you must know, that a Moral and unblameable Person, if he did not Herd with them, was an Abomination to that Party. I have heard one of the chiefest of them out of St. *Marys* Pulpit, deliver himself concerning them in this manner; *There's more hope of a Whoremonger a common Drunkard, a profane Swearer, than of these Moral Men; they justifie their selves; Do not we, say they, do our Exercises constantly, do we ever miss College Prayers? Are we out of the Town after* Tom *has Toll'd, and the College Gates shut? Do we Injure any body, do we not pay our Battles and Debts? Are we Drunkards, Swearers, or Whoremasters? Who can say black is our Eye? My Beloved, such are in a desperate Condition, Jesus Christ can take no hold upon such Persons*; and much more to this purpose.

Dr. *Ward* rid out this Storm, but Dr. *Wilkins* put into the Port of Matrimony, marrying the Protectors Sister, Widow of Dr. *Peter French*, a Canon of *Christ-Church*, who really was a Pious, Humble and Learned Person, and an excellent Preacher, and,

if

if I should say the best of all that Party, I should not give him more than his due praise; in a word, this Party were rigidly and unmercifully Censorious against the Moral Men, and fondly and ridiculously tender towards those of their own Communion: If a Woman happened to be got with-Child by a Moral Man, 'twas in him a reigning Sin; but if it was by a Church Member, 'twas a *failing, whereunto the best Saints were subject, not excepting the Man after Gods own heart.* This Matrimony of Dr. *Wilkins*, before-mentioned, did him good, Service at hand, gain'd him a strong Interest, and Authority in the University, and set him at safety, and out of the reach of his Adversaries, and also preserv'd the University from running into Disorder and Confusion; but after the Kings Return, it was for a while a Spoke in his Cart, and hinder'd his Preferment, as we shall make appear in its due place.

About this time the Headship of *Jesus College* became vacant, and by the direction of Dr. *Mansell*, the legal, but ejected Principal, who liv'd privately in that College, and by the Votes of the Fellows Dr. *Ward* was chosen and admitted Principal, but he

was

was thought too dangerous by the Ruling Party, and they complained of it to the Proctor; whereupon he, and the Fellows who chose him, were cited to appear at *White-Hall*, and being there, were severely reprimanded, and in particular Mr. *Vaughan*, Brother to the late Lord Chief Justice, and threatned to be all Expell'd, but Dr. *Ward* was treated with great Civility, and highly Complemented, and dismiss'd, not without promise of particular Favour. But he was no sooner return'd to *Oxford*, but he found there an Order to yield Possession to Mr. *Howell*, one of the other Party, and then Fellow of *Exeter College*, and he, I mean Dr. *Ward*, was promis'd upon so doing, a Stipend of Eighty pounds *per Annum*, which promise was never perform'd, and so he was defeated; but as all disappointments prov'd generally to his advantage, so did this also, for a short while after, he was not only chosen, and admitted, but enjoy'd a better Place. Dr. *Wilkins*, Dr. *Goddard*, and perhaps two or three more, whom I need not name, us'd their constant endeavour to oppose the Fury, and moderate the Heats of the fiery, giddy Party, and to advance the interest of Learning, and in

order

order to that, they concluded to get Dr.
Ward more firm rooting amongst them, and
did not despair of it, notwithstanding this
disappointment. But here it is necessary
for me to look a little backwards: In the
Year of our Lord 1649. Dr. *Kettle* President of *Trinity College* died; he was, as I
have heard, an honest Man, and a good
Governour, but in his latter time peevish,
and froward, and had never any great stock
of Learning. When *Oxford* was a Garrison
for King *Charles* the Martyr, he would stand
at the College Gate, and observe what Persons came to walk in *Trinity Grove*, for that
was then the *Oxford Hide-Park*, the Ren-
desvous of the Nobility and Gentry. I say,
he took notice of all, and usually had a
Saying to every one of them, which instead of vexing them, made them laugh,
then would tell the next of the Fellows he
chanc'd to see, I met some *Jack* Lords going into my Grove, but I think I have nettled
them, I gave them such entertainment they
little look'd for. At my first coming to
the University of *Oxford*, there were innumerable Bulls and Blunders father'd upon
him, as afterwards upon Dr. *Boldero* of *Cambridge*.

bridge. Upon Dr. *Kettles* death, the Fellows proceeded to an Election of a President, and it lay betwixt Mr. *Chillingworth*, a Person justly of great Fame for his Learning, and Dr. *Potter.* Mr. *Chillingworth* had the majority of Votes; but being then at a considerable distance from *Oxford*, and not able to come suddenly, and take Possession, Dr. *Potter* laid hold upon this advantage, and was admitted; in a short time after when the University was Visited, Dr. *Potter* was Ejected, and Dr. *Harris*, Rector of *Hanwell* in *Oxfordshire*, put into his place. This Dr. *Harris* was a very eminent Preacher, his Hair rather white than gray, his Speech Grave, Natural, and Pathetical; I never heard any Sermons which became the Persons who pronounc'd them, so well as his did him. After Dr. *Harris*'s decease, the Fellows chose Mr. *Hawes*, a Loyal, Learned and Modest Person, but of an infirm constitution of Health; he enjoy'd this Headship but a little time, and some days before his death resign'd it; whereupon Dr. *Ward*, to the great contentment and joy of the Moral, Sober Party, was elected President, which he accepted, and accordingly took

possession

possession of it. He us'd great diligence and care to put all things in order, and settle the troubled Affairs of it, governing with great Prudence and Reputation; but he continued in that Station a very little while, only till 1660, that memorable Year, for the happy Return of King *Charles* the Second, when he resign'd it to Dr. *Potter*; 'tis true, he left *Trinity College*, and *Oxford*, ἔκων ἀεκόντι δε θύμῳ, with an unwilling willingness, for he was contented with his Condition, and so pleas'd with a Collegial Life, and the Charms of that sweet place, that he would willingly have remain'd there the rest of his days, and in order to that, proffer'd Dr. *Potter* an Equivalent, which was refus'd, but yet, had he resolv'd to have kept it, he had not wanted sufficient ground to dispute the Title at Law; for tho' it must be confess'd, Dr. *Potter* was illegally turn'd out, yet he never had a Statutable right to that place, as is before made manifest. But Dr. *Ward* not being willing to contend, left it, and also resign'd his *Savilian* Professors Place, and retir'd to *London*; what he did there, shall be the Subject of the next Chapter.

CHAP.

CHAP. VIII.

Of Dr. Wards *being in* London.

WE have observ'd before, that all Disappointments which happened to Dr. *Ward*, even since his first ejection out of *Cambridge*, have prov'd to his advantage; but this last of not retaining the Presidentship of *Trinity College*, turn'd more notoriously not only to his private Emolument, but to the public good also: For had he kept that Headship, I mean been buried alive in *Trinity College*, hiding his glorious Light under that Bushel, *Exeter* and *Salisbury* could not have boasted of so good a Bishop, and Benefactor; the Church of *England* had wanted such a Pillar, and Asserter of its Rights, and the Poor the Houses and Benefactions he has provided for them; he might have publish'd more Treatises in Divinity, and Mathematics, but he could not possibly have done so much good.

On *May* the 29*th.* since made a perpetual Holiday by Act of Parliament, King *Charles* return'd in Glory to his Kingdoms, from
which

which he had been unjustly Exil'd for many
Years. He was no sooner fix'd in his
Throne, but he resolv'd to settle the Church,
as by the Ancient Laws Establish'd, to restore and to confirm it, all its Lands, Rights
and Privileges of which it had been Sacri-
legiously robb'd and despoil'd. To this
end, several new Bishops were Consecrated,
who, together with those who out-liv'd the
Storm of the Persecution, were commission'd
by the King to do it effectually. Those
Ministers who were ejected out of their
Livings for adhering to the King's Cause,
were restor'd, and notice was given to all
who had any pretension to any Ecclesiastical
Places or Dignities, at, or before such a
day, nominated, to appear, and enter their
Claims, for after that day the Commissioners intended to fill all the Vacancies in
the Churches. You may remember what
I said in the Fourth Chapter, that Bishop
Brounrig had conferr'd the Precentorship
of the Church of *Exeter* upon Dr. *Ward*
many Years before. And now that Title
which had lain so long dormant, and
as to outward appearance dead, awak'd,
reviv'd, and took place, and was accepted
by the Commissioners, by whose order he
was

was admitted Precentor, not long after he was chosen Dean, and in the same Year consecrated Bishop of *Exeter*. During these Transactions, Dr. *Ward* had frequent occasion to ride betwixt *London* and *Oxford*, which Journey he always perform'd in one day, upon a high-mettled, dancing, I might say, a run-away Mare, for almost any body besides him would have found her so; but he was indeed a good Horseman, and valu'd himself upon it. I have heard him say when he was a young Scholar in *Cambridge*, and us'd to ride in company of others to *London*, or elsewhere, he frequently chang'd Horses with those who could not make theirs go, and with those tir'd Jades lead the way; but this is to be reckon'd amongst the least of his Accomplishments. By so often taking this Journey in the heat of the Year, he threw himself into a dangerous Fever, and lay long sick of it in *Gresham-College*, which not being well Cur'd, by reason that Dr. *Goddard* his Fysician, was then very full of Employment, and could not give him due attendance; I say it was not well Cur'd, he having not Purg'd after it, as it was necessary, it left in him an ill constitution of Health during the rest of
his

his Life, and tho' he wrestled with it, and bore up against it for many Years, yet he could never subdue it; *Morbum tolerare potuit, superare vero non potuit.*

Upon the promotion of Dr. *Reynolds* to the Bishopric of *Norwich*, the Church of St. *Laurence Jewry* became Vacant, and it being in the Kings Gift, was conferr'd upon Dr. *Ward*, who kept it till he was nominated Bishop of *Exeter*, and upon his resignation procur'd it for his Friend Dr. *Wilkins*, who was at that time wholly destitute of all Employment and Preferment; for upon the Kings Restoration, and the new Modelling of the University of *Cambridge*, he lost the Mastership of *Trinity-College*, having no other Title to it than the Presentation of *Richard Cromwell* the short-liv'd Protector; however, he wrong'd no body, for the Incumbent was dead, and none pretended any Right or Claim to it. And as if Fortune took delight in persecuting of him, and to heap Afflictions upon Afflictions, not long after, I mean in that dreadful and almost Universal Conflagration of *London*, he lost not only his Books, an irreparable loss, as I my self have also since experienc'd, but the unsatiable and devouring Flames,

Flames, consum'd and reduc'd to Ashes all his Houshold-stuff, his House, and his Parsonage also. Add to this, he, I mean Dr. *Wilkins*, was out of favour, both at *White-Hall* and *Lambeth*, for his Marriage mentioned before in the Sixth Chapter; upon that account Archbishop *Shelden*, who had the Keys of the Church for a great time in his power, and could admit into it and keep out of it whom he pleas'd, I mean dispos'd of all Ecclesiastical Preferments, entertain'd a strong prejudice against him, so that he was now not only without any Place, but also without probability of obtaining one; so that his Fortune was as low as it could be, but he did not stay there long. I remember Bishop *Ward* told me at that time, I am much concern'd for your Brother, and write to him oftner than I otherwise should, to keep up his Spirits and assure him of my utmost assistance, for the bettering of his Condition, lest he should imagine that I, in my Prosperity, should be unmindful of him in Adversity. And these good words were soon followed with answerable Actions, he procur'd for him the Precentors place at *Exeter*, which was the first step he ascended towards a better Fortune; then

did

did also the Honourable Society of *Grays-Inn* make choice of him for their Lecturer, and not long after, upon the death of Bishop *Hall*, he was made Bishop of *Chester*, not only without, but against the Consent of the Archbishop of *Canterbury*. After which, Bishop *Ward* introduc'd him into the Archbishops presence and favour, who entertain'd him very obligingly, declaring that the prejudice he had against him was unjust, and if he had known him sooner, he would have been sooner preferr'd. Before Dr. *Wilkins* was settled in his Bishopric, a certain Person address'd himself to the Archbishop, and desir'd his Graces Recommendation to him for a Place in his Gift. *No*, reply'd the Archbishop, *that I can by no means do, it would be a very unreasonable thing in me, to desire a Favour from one whose Promotion I oppos'd*; and they ever afterwards kept a fair Correspondence. The two other Bishops continued their old Friendship till death, tho' it is not to be deny'd, that they afterwards differ'd in their Opinions concerning the Bill of Comprehension, the Bishop of *Salisbury* opposing it, and the Bishop of *Chester* with great zeal espousing it. Upon the translation of Bishop

shop *Gauden* to *Worcester*, Dr. *Ward*, without knowing any thing of it, by the Interest of the Duke of *Albemarle*, and Sir *Hugh Pollard*, then Controller, and some other of his Western Friends, whom he had oblig'd during his residence at *Exeter*, was nominated the Bishop thereof *An. Dom.* 1662. After he was compleated Bishop, he put all things in order to go to his Diocess, and reside there; accordingly he went to *Exeter*, whither we will accompany him, and relate what he did there in the next Chapter.

CHAP. IX.

Of his being Bishop of Exeter.

UPON his arrival at *Exeter*, he found all things in Disorder; the Bishops Palace was in the possession of a Sugar-Baker, and put to that sweet use; the Church was parted by a Traverse, the Presbyterians and Independants dividing it betwixt them, which Inconveniences the former Bishop took no care to remove, expecting to be translated to a better Bishopric, as afterwards he was. But before we speak of Dr.

Dr. *Ward* as a Bishop, give me leave to take a short view of what he did when he was Dean of *Exeter*. He first cast out of the Temple the Buyers and Sellers, who had usurp'd it, and therein kept distinct Shops to vent their Ware. At his Majestys Restoration the Nonconformists there being buoy'd up by some powerful Friends, who for their private Interest drove on, and hop'd to obtain a general Toleration of all Religions, excepting Popery, took the boldness to petition the King, that the Partition in the Cathedral might not be taken down, that they might enjoy *Altare contra Altare*. But to give them their due, they were so generous, as to allow one half of the Church to the use of the Episcopal Party, to whom all did of right belong, that therein Divine Service might be celebrated according to the Act of Parliament for Uniformity of Worship, reserving the other part to their selves to Meet and Hold-forth in; but their design was prevented by the early application of the Dean to the King and Council, from whom he procur'd an Order, to restore the Church to its ancient Form and Shape, and remove the Innovations; he accordingly caus'd the Partition to be pull'd down,

and

G

and repair'd and beautified the Cathedral, the Expenses whereof amounted to twenty five thousand Pounds; he also bought a new pair of Organs, esteem'd the best in *England*, which cost two thousand Pound. But it may be demanded, how came he by such vast Sums of Money? I answer, it was not done out of his private Purse, but out of the Church Revenues; for all the Leases belonging to that Ancient and Rich Church being expir'd, the renewing of them caus'd that plenty. But now let's consider him as Bishop: He first retriev'd the Palace out of the hands of the Sugar-Baker, whom his Predecessor found and left in quiet possession; he repair'd it, and made it habitable, for it was very ruinous, having been deserted before the Civil War, by the Bishops, who liv'd in other Houses; he took care of executing his Majestys Letters, commanding the Augmentation of poor Vicarages in that Diocese, and did it effectually; he also encreased the Prebends Stipends, from Four, to Twenty Pounds a Year: He kept his constant Trienial Visitations, in the first whereof he Confirm'd many thousands of all Ages and different Sexes; he also settled the Ecclesiastical Courts, and without

without any Noise or Clamour, reduc'd that
Active, Subtile, and then Factious People,
to great Conformity, not without the ap-
probation even of the Adversaries themselves. At this time *Falmouth*, from an inconsiderable Village, usually call'd *Penny-
come-quick*, being grown a great and beautiful Town, equal, if not superiour to *Truro*,
procur'd a Charter from King *Charles*,
wherein the new name of *Falmouth* was
establish'd, and a Penalty put upon those
who should call it by its old scandalous
Nick-name. The People of this New Town
had also built a stately Church, and sent
to the Bishop entreating him to Consecrate
it, which he did, dedicating it to the blessed
Memory of King *Charles* the Martyr, having first taken care, that about a hundred
pound *per annum* should be settled for the
maintenance of the Minister. During his
residence at *Exeter*, he gain'd the love of
all the Gentry, and had particularly the
help and countenance of the Duke of *Albemarle*, who in all things shew'd himself
most ready to assist him in the execution
of his Jurisdiction. The Bishop did not
leave *Exeter* till he had made that Bishopric
better than he found it, which he did by
                                        procuring

procuring the Deanery of St. *Burien*, near the Lands-end in *Cornwal*, to be settled upon the Bishops of *Exeter* for ever, by the Kings Letters Patents, after the death of Dr. *Weeks*, who then was the Incumbent; he did not this to profit himself, for he had no prospect of ever being the better for it, 'twas only for the pleasure of doing good: It did not become void till Bishop *Sparrows* time, who was Bishop *Wards* immediate Successor; he first enjoy'd it, and it does still, and I hope ever will continue in the possession of the Bishops of *Exeter*, and their Successors.

Dr. *Thomas Wykes* the last Dean of St. *Burien*, was heretofore Chaplain to Archbishop *Laud*, I have often seen his Name to the Licensing of Books particularly to *Ovids Metamorfosis* Translated by Mr. *Sandys*, and Printed *Anno Dom.* 1640. He had Wit enouf, but it was not in a wise Mans keeping, as it often happens; this appears by an Answer he gave to King *Charles* the First when he was in *Cornwal*, in the time of the Civil Wars. The Doctor being well mounted, and near his Majesty, the King spoke thus to him, *Doctor you have a pretty Nag under you, I pray how Old is he?* To

which

which he, out of the abundance of the
Quibbles of his heart, return'd this Answer;
*If it please your Majesty, he is now in the
Second Year of his Reign*, pleasing himself
with the ambiguity of the sound of that
word, signifying either Kingship or Bridle.
The good King did not like this unmannerly Jest, and gave him such an Answer
as he deserv'd, which was this; *Go, you are
a Fool.* While the Bishop was at *Exeter*,
as he told me at my return from *Italy*, he
receiv'd a Letter from me, dated at *Rome*;
when there were some of the Church and
Citizens with him, he craved leave to open
and read it, and when he had done put it
up into his Pockets; then some of the Company took occasion to ask him whence it
came; he replyed, *from* Pope *at* Rome.
In a trice it was buzz'd abut the City, that
the Bishop was a Papist, and held Correspondence with the Pope; and this would
have been believed, and have past for cur-
rent amongst those who rejoyce to hear ill
of Bishops, if he had not timely undeceiv'd
them. Upon the Exaltation of Bishop *Shel-
don* to the See of *Canterbury*, Doctor *Hench-
man* Bishop of *Salisbury*, was translated to
London, and Dr. *Alexander Hide*, a Kinsman

of

of the Chancellor, from being Dean of *Salisbury* was made Bishop thereof upon his death, for he enjoy'd it but a small time. The Bishop of *Exeter* by the Kings favour, was made Bishop of *Salisbury A. Dom.* 1666. After the Ceremony of the Translation was over, he set forward for *Salisbury*; I waited on him at his first going thither as Bishop, and spent much time with him there. He was very acceptable to his Diocese, innumerable Persons coming in throngs to meet him, and striving who should be forwardest in shewing him Respect; but what was more remarkable, the tide of their Love and Affection for him was not then at the highest, but still flow'd and encreas'd as long as he liv'd, as we shall make appear in the next Chapter.

CHAP. X.

Of his being Bishop of Salisbury.

AFter his public Entry and Reception, which was as great as the place could afford, the Mayor and Aldermen in their Formalities welcoming him, the School-masters of the two Free Schools at the head of of their Scholars Congratulating him, two choice Boys pronouncing Latin Orations upon that Subject, full of his Praises, and declaring how happy they esteem'd their selves to have such a Bishop, sent them as it were from Heaven. His first care was to beautifie and repair the Cathedral, tho' it did not want much reparation; for to the eternal Honour of the Loyal Gentry of that Diocese, whose Names I wish I knew, that I might, as much as in me lies, Consecrate them to Posterity, during the whole time of the Civil Wars and the Kings Exile, when there was neither Bishop nor Dean to take care of it, they employ'd Workmen to keep that Sacred and Magnificent Pile in repair. I have been told by some who then liv'd in *Salisbury*, that they have several times seen Men at Work, sometimes on the inside of the Church, and otherwhiles on the outside; and asking them, by whom they were set on Work, receiv'd this Answer; *They who employ'd us will pay us, trouble not your selves to inquire who they are, whoever they are, they do not desire to have their Names known.* There being therefore not much to be done as to the reparation, he employ'd himself in the Decoration of the Cathedral:

Cathedral: First, at his proper Charges, Paving the Cloyster, I mean that side of it which leads out of his Garden into the Church. At his Exhortation, and more than proportionable expence, the Pavement of the Church was mended where it was faulty, and the whole Quire laid with white and black Squares of Marble, the Bishops, Deans, and all the Prebendaries Stalls made New and Magnificent, and the whole Church was kept so clean, that any one who had occasion for Dust to throw upon the Superscription of a Letter, he would have a hard task to find it there. I have seen many Metropolitan Churches, but never any, nay, not that glorious Fabrique of St. *Peters* at *Rome*, which exceeds the imagination of all those who have not beheld it, was kept so neat as this in his time: Nay, the Sacrifice therein was as pure; there might be heard excellent Preaching, and Divine Service celebrated, with exemplary Piety, admirable Decency, and Celestial Music. His next care was to repair, I might almost say rebuild his Palace, which was much ruin'd, the Hall being pull'd down, and the greatest part of the House converted to an Inn, having a Passage o-
pen'd

pen'd thro' the Close Wall to give Entrance to the Market People, and other Travellers who came thro' *Harnham* from the Western parts; what remain'd of the Palace was divided into small Tenements, and let out to poor Handicraft-men. This dilapidation and spoil was the work of one *Van Ling* a Dutch-man, by Trade a Taylor, who bought it of the Parliament, when Bishops Lands were expos'd to Sale: *See Salisbury Canto*, Part 1. *Stanza* 20. His Expences in altering, repairing, and rebuilding, amounted to above two Thousand Pounds, there being little or nothing done in order to it by his Predecessors, who had the Cream of the Bishopric. While he was thus employ'd, I remember he came to me one morning and desir'd me to take a turn in the Church with him, he having a private way, as I have said before, thro' his Garden and the Cloysters; when we were enter'd, *Come*, said he to me, *which think you will be the most convenient place for me to be buried in? Oh my Lord*, said I, *may that day be far off. Come, come*, said he, *tell me your opinion, for I am in earnest.* Whereupon we view'd several places, and at last agreed upon that wherein he now lies interr'd; so

that

that it is not true of him, what *Horace* said of a Noble Roman in his time, *Struis domos, Immemor Sepulchri.* i. e. *You build Palaces and are unmindful of your Grave.* While he was Bishop of *Exeter*, he had made, as I may call it, the *Notitiæ* of that Bishoprick, with no small pains and industry, which he bestow'd, upon his removal to *Salisbury*, upon Bishop *Sparrow* his Successor; which prov'd not only an ease, but a light and guide to him in the management of his Affairs. After he settled at *Salisbury*, he began, and in a short time finish'd such another Book for that Diocese, wherein were particulariz'd all the Rectories and Vicarages in that Bishoprick, all the Patrons Names, with their undoubted and disputable Titles; as also the Names of all the Incumbents, with their several qualifications, as to Conformity, or Nonconformity, Learning, or Ignorance, peaceable, or contentious Conversation, Orthodox or Heretical Opinion, good or scandalous Lives; for all which he had fram'd peculiar Marks, which he shew'd and explain'd to me: He found by daily experience, that this stood him in great stead, and did him eminent service: For when any Clergy-man of his Diocese came

came to him, as soon as he heard his Name,
he knew his Character, and could give a
shrewd guess at his business, and so was out
of danger of being surprizd. He had not
been long thus employd, after his arrival
at *Salisbury*, when he was seizd with a violent Looseness, and a Scorbutical Atrofie,
for which, by Dr. *Sydenhams* advice, he betook himself to riding upon *Salisbury* Plains,
which he continued the latter part of the
Summer, all the Autumn, and as often as the
Weather permitted in Winter: That he
might perform this Exercise with more
convenience, and not neglect the Affairs of
his Bishopric, he borrowed a House of the
Earl of *Abington* at *Bishops-Lavington*, situated in a pleasant and healthful Air, near
the End of the Plains Northward of *Salisbury*, and the Center of *Wiltshire*, and so more
convenient for any of that County who
had business with him, than *Salisbury*; it
was also about four miles distant from the
Devizes, a good Market-Town. Hence he
set out every day, except *Sundays*, if the
Weather permitted, nay, and sometimes
when it was not seasonable, for we have
been often caught in Storms of Rain and
Snow, and forcd to seek shelter on the
Lee-

Lee-side of the next Hay-Rick we could gallop to: We us'd to ride ten miles forwards or *tantamount* by our Watches, before we returnd, and after Dinner, we repeated the same, or the like Journey. The Bishop continued this Exercise, till upon account he had travelld more than three thousand miles. The longer he rid, the stronger he grew, so that he did not only tire me, but even the Grooms and Servants who usd to attend him, that he has sometimes been forcd to content himself with the Company of one of his meanest Servants. This Exercise set him right, and I may truly say, it was the only time that ever any Fysicians *Recipe* did him good; yet he was a great lover of them and their Prescriptions, and very Liberal, I may say Prodigal in his Fees to them: He also delighted much in Fysic Books, which wrought the Effect upon him, which they usually do upon Hypocondriacal Persons, that is, made him fancy that he had those Diseases which he there found describd, and accordingly take Remedies for them. He would take Pills and Potions when he had no need of them, from which, not only I endeavourd to divert him, telling him 'twas spending the

the Ammunition before the Town was besiegd, but even Mr. *Eyres* his Apothecary,
a very honest and skilful Person, who died
Mayor of *Salisbury*, has joynd with me in
that request, even against his own Interest.

To keep his Diocese in Conformity, he
took great care to settle able Ministers in the
great Market and Borough Towns, as
Reading, *Abingdon*, *Newbery*, the *Devizes*,
Warminster, &c. and because they are for
the most part Vicarages of small value, as
Prebends in the Church fell void, he bestowd them on the Ministers of these
Towns. He also us'd his endeavour to sup-
press Conventicles, which so angerd that
Party, that in the Year 1669. they forgd
a Petition against him, under the Hands
of some chief Clothiers, pretending that
they were Molested, and their Trade ruind,
and that some of them imployd a Thousand Men, others eight Hundred, and that
this Persecution took away the Livelihood
of eight Thousand Men, Women and Children. But it was made appear at the
Council-Table, that this Petition was a notorious Libel, and that none of those there
mentiond to be Persecuted and Ruind,
were so much as Summond into the Ecclesiastical

siastical Court; as also, that many whose Names were subscribd to that Petition, knew nothing of it: So that instead of lessening the Bishops Favour with the King, they augmented it. Let this be said once for all, he was no Violent Man, nor of a Persecuting Spirit, as these Petitioners represented him; but if at any time he was more active than ordinary against the Dissenters, it was by express Command from the Court, sometimes by Letters, and sometimes given in Charges by the Judges of the Assizes, which Councils alterd frequently; now in favour of the Dissenters, and then again in opposition to them; as it is well known to those who livd then, and had the least insight into public Affairs. 'Tis true, he was for the Act against Conventicles, and labour'd much to get it pass, not without the Order and Direction of the greatest Authority, both Civil and Ecclesiastical, not out of Enmity to the Dissenters Persons, as they unjustly suggested, but of Love to the repose and welfare of the Government; for he believd if the growth of them were not timely suppressed, it would either cause a necessity of a standing Army to preserve the Peace, or a general Toleration

tion, which would end in Popery, whither
all things then had an apparent tendancy.
That Act had this Effect, it shewd the Dissenters were not so numerous and considerable as they gave themselves out to be,
designing thereby to make the Government
believe it was impracticable to quell them;
for where this Act was duely executed, it
put an end to their Meetings, as it was
evident in his Diocese; for in *Salisbury* there
was not one Conventicle left, and but a few
in the skirts of *Wiltshire*, bordering upon
Somerset-shire, where for want of a settled
Militia, by reason of the non-age of the
Duke of *Somerset*, the Lord-Lieutenant of
that County, they sometimes met in Woods,
but upon Complaint their Meetings were
suppressed, and his Majesty was pleasd to
own and accept this as good Service to the
Publick, and to incourage the Bishop in it.
But a little after, I know not upon what
ground, the Weather-Cock of the Court-
Council turnd to the contrary Point, and one
BLOUD, a Person notorious for stealing the
Crown out of the *Tower*, and offering that
barbarous violence to the Duke of *Ormond*,
being of a sudden become a great Favourite
at Court, and the chief Agent of the Dissenters;

ters; this *BLOUD*, I say, brought the Bishop of *Salisbury* a verbal Message from the King, not to Molest the Dissenters; upon which he went to wait on his Majesty, and humbly represented to him, that there were only two troublesom Nonconformists in his Diocese, whom he doubted not, with his Majesty's permission, but that he should bring to their Duty, and then he named them. *These are the very Men*, replyed the King, *you must not meddle with*; to which he obey'd, letting the Prosecution against them fall.

CHAP. XI.

Concerning the Bishops Hospitality.

BIshops are commanded by St. *Paul* to be Hospitable; never did any yield more punctual obedience to that Apostolical Injunction, than this Bishop of *Salisbury* did; for, be it spoken without any reflection, no Person in that County, or the Diocese, that ever I heard of, kept constantly so good a Table as he did, which also as occasion requir'd, was augmented. He usd

to

to say, that he expected all his Brethren of the Clergy, who upon any business came to *Salisbury*, should make use of his Table, and that he took it kindly of all the Gentry who did so. Scarce any Person of Quality pass'd betwixt *London* and *Exeter*, but if their occasions permitted, Din'd with him. The meanest Curates were welcome to his Table, and he never fail'd to drink to them, and treat them with all affability and kindness imaginable. He often told his Guests, they were welcome to their own, for he accounted himself but their Steward. Never was there a more hearty Entertainer; I have heard him say, 'Tis not kind nor fair, to ask a Friend that visits you, Will you drink a Glass of Wine? For besides, that by this Question you discover your inclination to keep your Drink, it also leads a modest Guest to refuse it tho' he desires it: You ought to call for Wine, drink to him, fill a Glass and present it; then, and not till then, it will appear whether he had any inclination to drink or not. When any Persons of greater quality than himself came to *Salisbury*, as there not infrequently did in their way to *Ireland*, he went to their Lodgings and invited them himself,

himself, and never fail'd to Treat them very splendidly. He knew not who Din'd with him, unless, as I said just now, they were of his own Invitation, till he saw them at the Table. After Morning Prayers, which he seldom, unless upon urgent occasions, miss'd; he constantly walk'd up to his Chamber, and stay'd there till a Servant brought word that Dinner was upon the Table. After Dinner, if any extraordinary Company were present, he would stay with them, drink a Dish or two of Coffee or Tea, while they, who had a mind to it, drank Wine, whereof there was plenty, and of the best. When the Bell *Tilld*, to use the *Salisbury* Frase, to Evening Prayers, then he call'd for his Habits and went to Church, carrying with him, for the most part, all the Company, who were obligd to go to Prayers with him out of Civility, if not Devotion. Besides what he gave away at the Palace-Gate, where he constantly re-lievd a great number of Poor, he inquird after those the French call *Paures honteaux*, who wanted and were ashamd to beg, and sent them Money to their Houses. He had also a Band of Pensioners, if I may so

call

call them, the number whereof were limited, but I do not remember of how many
it consisted; these were payd Weekly, and
as one dy'd another was substituted in his
place; and those poor People who could
get their selves lifted in this Troop, count-
ed their selves sufficiently provided for, if
not for their own, yet for the Bishops Life,
for the continuation thereof they dayly and
heartily put up their Petitions. He never
went to take the Air, which he usd to do
very frequently, but he gave liberally to
the Poor, not staying till they askd, 'twas
enouf if they stood in the way, or casually
met him on the Plains; nay I have often
seen him call those who were at a distance
from him and expected nothing, and give
them Money. When his Coach, or if he
went out a Horseback, or any of his Retinue appeard in *Harnham*, thro' which we
usually passd to the *Hare-Warren*, all the
Children would immediately leave their
Play and cry out, *My Lord Bishop is coming,
my Lord Bishop is coming*: Upon which A-
larm, all the poorer Inhabitants appear at
their doors, praying God to bless his Lordship, and receivd his Alms. He never
went

went from *Salisbury* to *London*, or upon his
Visitation, but he was accompanied part of
his way by many of the Citizens, I may
say of all, who either had Horses of their
own, or could procure them for Love or
Money, wishing him a happy Journey, a
speedy and safe return. Both at his going
forth, and returning back to the City, all
the way from the Palace to the Close-Gate,
usd to be lind with regiments of Poor,
many whereof upon their Knees, with their
Hands elevated to Heaven, loudly, and I
dare say, devoutly and heartily, praying
God, either for his good Journey, or praising
him for his return in safety: I write not
this by *hear-say*, but as an Eye and Ear witness, and that not once only, but very frequently. I have said before, he often rode
out for his Health, and when we were upon the Plains, I say We, for I was his *Fidus
Achates*, as constant to him as the Shadow
to the Body; sometimes we by chance chopt
upon the Dogs, and sometimes by my con-
trivance, knowing whereabouts they intended to Hunt, but however, and whenever it
happened, the Bishop would ride a Ring or
two very briskly, but when it came to Pick-
ing

ing work, or Cold Hunting, he would leave
them, and proceed in his Promenade; but
first I was sent to invite all the Gentlemen
to Dine with him, whether he knew them
or not; and this not once only, but *Toties
quoties*, as long as his Health permitted.
Our Airing was usually to a Hedge in
Shaftsbury Road, about ten mile distant
from *Salisbury*, thence we returnd and
reachd home by Dinner time. Yet notwithstanding his hospitable way of living,
and splendid treating of Persons of Quality,
his Alms, his private and public Benefactions, of which we shall treat in the next
Chapter, I may boldly and truly say, there
never was in that, or any other Episcopal
See, so careful a Steward, for so he us'd
to term himself, or so good a manager of
the Episcopal Demeans. I have heard him
say, If these Lands had been mine own,
either by Purchase or Inheritance, I could
not have been so solicitous to preserve them
from damage. He had good Woods about
six or seven mile from *Salisbury*, of which
he cut down annually only so much as he
made use of in repairing or building the
Palace, and sold only so much as defrayd
                                          the

the price of the Coals which he burnt in his Kitchin; neither would he suffer one Stick to be cut down for any other purpose, tho' often solicited thereunto. I remember he told me, I am resolvd, who ever succeeds me, shall have no occasion to be sorry that I was his Predecessor in this Bishopric, for I will leave it better than I found it; and he did not fail to be as good as his word, as we shall make manifest in the next Chapter. He us'd once every Year, and sometimes oftner, ride to the Woods above-mentiond and visit all the Coppices, and ask the Woodward several Questions, and give him strict charge concerning the *Mounds, Fences,* &c. *But for all this,* said he to me, for I always accompanied him when ever he rid out, *these Fellows may easily Cheat me, but I suppose my frequently coming hither, unawares to them, and seeming so inquisitive, will make them more cautious.* To shew his care yet farther, even when the Kings Commissioners came to *Salisbury* to buy Timber for the Royal Navy, he would not consent to the felling of one Tree, till he had received the Kings express Orders for so doing.

CHAP.

CHAP. XII.

Concerning his Acts of Charity.

WE have declard in the Ninth Chapter what he did for the Church of *Exeter*, I mean his procuring the Deanery of St. *Burien*, to be annext to the Bishops of that Place. It is our work now, to shew what good he did to the Bishopric and City of *Salisbury*, and whether he left them better than he found them. He was very kind to the City, granting them what ever they desird of him, and in particular, his Picture at full length in his Garter Robes, the work of Mr. *John Greenhill*, who was a Scholar of Sir *Peter Lelies*, an excellent Painter; this Piece is set up in the Town House, and esteem'd as an inestimable Relic. He also renewd to the City a Lease of the Mansion-House, and some Lands, which were formerly my Lord *Awdleys*, Earl of *Castle-Haven* in *Ireland*, which, for that Lords committing Crimes not fit to be nam'd, and being Convicted and Executed, became forfeited to the Crown, and so fell

to

to the Bishop, to whom all Forfeitures are granted by the Kings Letters Patents. For doing this, he would accept of no other gratuity than a pair of Gloves, as an acknowledgment. He also contributed largely towards making their River Navigable, not only with his Money, but Advice, and dug the first Spadeful himself when they began that Work. He also made several Journeys in their behalf to the King and Council, and answerd the Objections which several *Hampshire* Gentlemen made against it, as I have briefly mention'd in the *Salisbury Canto*, Part 1. Stanza 23. To the Bishopric of *Salisbury* he was also a great Benefactor, by prevailing with the King to annex and unite to it for ever, that Honourable and not unprofitable Place, the Chancelorship of the most Noble Order of the Garter, the Ensigns whereof are, a Medal of Gold hanging upon a Chain of the same Metal, and he was the first Protestant Bishop who had the honour to wear it. And here I think it will not be impertinent to give a short History of this Office. The first Chancellor of the Garter was Bishop *Beauchamp, Anno Dom.* 1450, and that Honour was enjoy'd by his Successors the Bishops

shops of *Salisbury*, till the time of Cardinal *Campeggio*, who having incurrd the displeasure of King *Henry* the Eighth for differing from him in the matter of the Divorce, retird to *Rome*, and died there, *A. D.* 1539. and lies buried in the Church of *Santa Maria Tras Tevere*. Then had the Bishops of *Salisbury* enjoyd that Honour Eighty nine Years, since which time it has always been in the hands of Laymen, till it pleasd King *Charles* the Second, upon the humble petition and claim of Dr. *Ward*, to restore it to him and his Successors the Bishops of *Salisbury* for ever, after the death of Sir *Henry de Vic*, the last Lay-Chancellor, and after it had been out of the See one hundred thirty and two Years: The Letters Patent bear date *Novemb.* 25. *Anno Domini* 1671. He was also very forward and liberal in promoting any good design in the way of Learning, as Dr. *Castle* in his Epistle Dedicatory before his Learned *Lexicon* testifies, in these words. *Enimvero universæ hæ literæ, plus minus septingentas libras tantum mihi porrexerunt, ad promovendum opus, in quo millenas plures infaustus exhausi, præter plurima, atque ingentia valde, quæ contraxi debita, Quid quod prænominatæ Collectæ summæ pars*
maxima,

maxima, quadringenta scilicet libræ, procuratione atque opera solertissima prudentissimaque Reverendi admodum in Deo Patris Sethi Domini Episcopi Sarisburiensis, intra quatuordecem dies suerant conquisitæ. That is,

But all these, speaking of the Kings, the Archbishops and other Bishops Commendatory Letters, *produced me but seven hundred pound, a little more or less, and that to promote a Work wherein I had spent some thousands, besides contracting some very great Debts. The major part of which Collection,* viz. *Four hundred pound, was procur'd for me in fourteen days, by the care and diligence of the Right Reverend Father in God* Seth *Lord Bishop of* Salisbury. I have heard the Bishop speak with pleasure concerning this Collection, saying, the four hundred pound was contributed by the Clergy of the Dioceses of *Exeter* and *Salisbury* only; but his Modesty would not permit him to tell me what proportion thereof he gave. But the greatest and most seasonable Act of Charity, and public Benefaction, was building and endowing that Noble Pile, I mean the College of Matrons, for the entertainment and maintenance of Ten Widows of Orthodox Clergymen. I have often heard him express

press

press his dislike, if any one call'd it an Hospital; for, said he, many of these are well descended, and have liv'd in good reputation; I would not have it said of them, that they were reduc'd to an Hospital, but retird to a College, which has a more honourable sound. He accounted himself fortunate in purchasing Free Land whereupon to erect this Fabric, and yet more fortunate, that it was in the Close; for had it lain any where else, he must have been at the charges of a greater Structure, and endowing a Chapter, which was now needless, the Cathedral being so near, whereunto they might with ease, and were all of them engaged to repair both Morning and Evening, and stay out the whole time of Prayers, under a pecuniary penalty. During his Life he put in the Widows himself, and at his Death, he left a Catalogue of the Names of others whom he knew, or by the recommendation of others, believ'd to be fit objects of his Charity, these were next in succession, and afterwards the Election was to be in the Dean and Chapter, and the Bishop of *Salisbury*, *Alternis vicibus*, by turns. This College of Matrons is a strong regular Building, within the Close of *Salisbury*, and

a

a great Ornament to it. It is fitted for the reception of Ten Women, the Widows of Orthodox Ministers of the Diocese of *Salisbury*; and in case there should not be found so many therein, their vacancy is to be supplied out of the Bishopric of *Exeter*, but I fear this will never happen. They have each two Chambers and a little Garden peculiar to their selves. To the maintenance thereof the Bishop settled more than two hundred pounds a year in Free Land, which lies in the Neighbourhood; over the Gate is written in Letters of Gold, the Inscription following.

D°. O°. M°.
Collegium hoc Matronarum
Humillime Dedicavit
Sethus Episcopus Sarum
Anno Domini
MDCLXXXII.

That is,

To the Honour of Almighty God
This College of Matrons
Was most humbly Dedicated
By Seth *Bishop of Salisbury,*
In the Year of our Lord
1 6 8 2.

Two

Two Years after he built an Hospital at *Buntingford* in *Hertford-shire*, the place of his Nativity, for Ten poor aged Men, allowing each of them Ten pound *per annum*, which is also a Noble Structure, and bears this Inscription.

Anno Domini 1684.
*This Hospital was Erected and Endowed
By* Seth Ward, *Doctor of Divinity,
Lord Bishop of* Salisbury, *and
Chancellor of the most Noble Order
Of the Garter.
Who was Born in this Town, within the
Parish of* Aspenden, *and Educated
In the Free-School of* Buntingford.

These poor Men are put in by Mr. *Freeman* and his Heirs for ever. Besides this, he augmented the Stipend of the Minister and the School-Master in that Town.

Tho' I am conscious that I have not ennumerated all his Benefactions, yet I will conclude this Chapter with his Erecting of four Scholarships at *Christs-College* in *Cambridge*, and endowing them with   pound *per Annum*, which in that University is a considerable Allowance, the Scholarships there

there being generally inferiour to those at *Oxford*, as the Fellowships better. He had designd to have placd this his Benefaction at *Sidney-College*, but upon some disgust altered his intention, tho it is not improbable but that that College might refuse his proffer upon very good Reasons: For at *Oxford* no College will accept a Benefaction which only increases the number of Fellows, or Scholars, for thereby the Society is rather injured, than profited, unless the Benefactor also builds Chambers for their reception; for taking away so many Chambers, takes away from the Fellows so many Pupils; but on the contrary, a Benefactor who will increase the Stipends of the Members of the Society, will always be very gratefully embraced.

C H A P. XIII.

Of his Friends.

SHould I enumerate all his Friends whom I knew, I must fill two or three Leaves with Names and Titles, and this Chapter would look like a Money Act, wherein the Commissioners were all particularly

cularly set down. I shall not therefore use
that dry way, I will insert but few, and
those distributed into several Classes; according to the laudable Custom of *England*,
giving Precedence to the Female Sex, and
placing them in the Van. Even from his
unjust expulsion out of *Cambridge*, which
we have mentioned in its due place, he
never was destitute of Friends of the fair
Sex, till some few Years before his Death,
never without proffers of Wives, much beyond his deserts; as the Markets go in
Smithfield, to several of whom, he, to my
knowledge, recommended good Husbands,
and his recommendation was effectual; of
these I will mention but one, for whom
he also procured a good Parsonage, and he
shall be Mr. *Gibson*, a Contemporary, a
Fellow-Collegian and Fellow-sufferer in the
Common Cause; he many Years after,
when his Children were like Olive Branches
about his Table, came from *Hertford-shire*
to *Salisbury* to give the Bishop a Visit, and
accosted him in this manner: 'My Lord, I
'am come to wait upon your Lordship, and
'to return my most humble and hearty
'Thanks for your many and great Kindnesses
'to me, I owe all to you, you have got me
　　　　　　　　　　　　　　　　　'all

'all that I have in this World, except my
'Children. The reason why he did not Marry
then, as I have received from himself, was this;
he had not an Estate or Preferment sufficient
to maintain a Wife suitable to the Fortunes
which was profferd with them. And that
he would not put it into the power of any
Woman, if they should happen to disagree,
as there are few, very few, if any Marriages
without Dissentions, those being the happiest
where they are less frequent, to upbraid
him that she had made him a Man, and
that had it not been for what she brought,
he would not have been worth a Groat.
Being made a Bishop, first of *Exeter*, and
afterwards of *Salisbury*, and consequently become greater and richer, 'tis not to be
imagin'd those proffers should diminish, I
am certain they increased; I knew several
Persons of great Quality and Estates, who
found ways to make it known to him, that
if he would address himself to them in the
honorable way of Marriage, he should not
want a kind entertainment. But at that time
he was furnished with another reason to continue in Celebacy; he thought it not un-
lawful, but undecent, for a Bishop to Marry; perhaps he had in his eye the Fate of
one

one of his Predecessors, Bishop *Jewell*, who married after he was Bishop of *Salisbury*, and upon that account received so severe a Reprimand from his Brother the Archbishop of *Canterbury*, and laid it so much to heart, that it accelerated his death. Upon these reasons he continued unmarried till his death. But this rare Example has been followed by none of his Profession, except only Dr. *Barrow*, as we shall have occasion to shew hereafter. 'Tis time now to take my leave of the Ladies, and proceed. While Bp. *Ward* resided at *Exeter*, *George* Duke of *Albemarle* began his Friendship with him, which continued, and augmented till his Graces death; he did him many good Offices at Court, and defended him against the Clamours and Calumnies of the Fanatics. The Bishop also was serviceable to the Duke, he instructed his Son in the Mathematics, he also waited upon him frequently while he was in Health, and was never absent from him in his Sickness; he was with him in the last moments of his Life, he gave him the Holy Sacrament, closd his Eyes, and preachd his Funeral Sermon, which was printed, both by it self, and amongst his Works, published by *James Collins* as above-mentioned.

I

mentioned. To him I will add the Earl of *Sandwich*, Vice-Admiral of *England*, who was his Contemporary in *Cambridge*, a great lover and very well skilld in the Mathematics, but most famous for his skill in Maritime Affairs, for his not only adventuring, but sacrificing his Life for his Country. The next shall be my Lord Chancellor *Hide*, who had the Bishop in great esteem, and treated him with intimate Familiarity. I remember when we were at *Astrop* Wells, he sent the Bishop a pleasant Letter by his youngest Son, wherein amongst other things, he strictly enjoyns not to infuse any Mathematics into him, for fear they should render him unfit to be a Politician. To which the Bishop return'd in answer, That he would obey his Lordships Commands, and principally because *De Wit* was a famous Instance, That a good Mathematician could not be an able Statesman. The Gentleman who brought this Letter, together with my Lord *Faulkland*, my Lord *Roxborough*, and several other of the Nobility of *England* and *Scotland*, perished in the memorable Shipwrack of the *Gloucester*, which was then carrying the

Duke

Duke of *York* to *Scotland*, upon the *Lemane Ore*, on *Friday May* 5. 1682.

This Story is so wonderful and honourable for the English Seamen that I cannot forbear telling it here; 'tis an amazing thing, that Mariners who are usually as rough as the Element they converse in, when in evitable Death was before their eyes and to be incurred within a very few minutes; that Mariners, I say, should have that presence of Mind, that inestimable value and deference for the Duke of *York*, as being of the Blood-Royal, and Brother to their King, as to take care of his safety and neglect their own, to put him into a Boat, and permit no other Persons to enter into it, but those he called out of the sinking Ship, for fear of over-lading it, and as soon as they perceiv'd the Boat clear of the Ship, and the Prince out of danger, that they all of them should throw up their Caps, and make loud Acclamations and Huzzas of Joy, as if they had obtained some signal Victory over their Enemies, and in this rapture sink to the bottom immediately, at the same instant concluding their Lives and their Jubilation. Many Reflections may be made upon this remarkable Story, but I being

being in haste, leave that work to others.

I cannot positively determine, whether my Lord *Clarendon* was in earnest, and believed that Mathematics would render those who understood them, unfit to manage State Affairs; but if he did, I put into the Scale against him another great Man, and Politician, I mean the late Duke of *Lauderdale*, who has often declar'd in the presence of divers Persons of Quality, from some of which I had it, that in his opinion the Bishop of *Salisbury* was the best Speaker in the House of Lords. I will muster but one more, that shall be *Anthony* Earl of *Shaftsbury*, who was for a considerable time a great Friend to our Bishop; they enterchanged many Visits, as they might conveniently do, their Houses in the Country being but at a small distance one from the other, and often consulted about Public Affairs; nay, after they went several ways in Parliament, tho their Intimacy was at end, yet their mutual Esteem continued: I have seen a printed Speech of the Earls, wherein he Treats the Bishop very honourably, preferring his Speeches before the rest of his Opponents, as having more of Argument in them, and being closer to the purpose.

CHAP.

CHAP. XIV.

A Continuation of the former.

IF I should persist in this way of enumerating the Bishops Friends*;   Dr. *Lluellyn.*
There's one, there's two, and so on like
Faggots, I should tire the Reader and my Self;
therefore as to those that remain, I shall
serve them up in Clusters, excepting two
or three, concerning whom I intend to treat
more at large. The Bench of Bishops had
that esteem for him, that they selected him
to observe and reply to the Earl of *Shafts-*
bury, if he should move any thing to the
detriment of the Church; for this Earl was
a Person of great Ability, and had a peculiar Talent to promote or hinder any thing
passing the House of Peers. To mount a
step higher, our Bishops Probity, Wisdom,
and Ability to manage the great and Ardu-
ous Affairs of State, was in so great esteem
for a considerable while, that he was spoke
of both at Court, and in the City, as the
fittest Person to supply the place of the
Archbishop of *Canterbury,* Lord-Keeper, or
Lord-

Lord-Treasurer, if any of them should become vacant. And I am confident it pleased him more to be esteemd worthy of such Trusts, than to have enjoyd the best of them. I well remember the time, when he told me, he had the proffer of the Bishopric of *Durham*, after Bishop *Cousins* death. Pray my Lord, said I, accept it, we shall have brave Horses there, and the long Journey betwixt *Bishops-Auclands* and *London*, will conduce much to the meliorating of your Health. He replied, I just now enterd it in my blue Book, that this day I refusd it. I replied, and pray my Lord, why did you so? *Because*, said he, *I did not like the Conditions*; but what they were, it would have been unmannerly for me to inquire, and he did not think it convenient to tell me. This his refusing so rich a Bishopric, is so great an Act of Self-denial, that I have reason to fear, 'twill not be credited upon my single Testimony; I shall therefore call in another Witness, against whom there can be no Exception, to corroborate mine; he shall be no lesser a Person than the present Bishop of *Durham*, whom not long after I met at *Reading*, being then there with the Bishop of *Salisbury*

in

in his Visitation, I having had the honour to have been acquainted with the Bishop of *Durham*, even from his first admission into *Lincoln College* in *Oxford*, laid hold on this occasion to felicitate his promotion to *Durham*: He replied, *'Twas proffered to your Bishop*, meaning the Bishop of *Salisbury*, *but he did not think fit to accept of it*. And here now I should add the Nobility and Gentry of *Wiltshire*, *Berkshire*, *Devonshire* and *Cornwal*, whose Diocesan he had been, but I remember my promise, to ease both the Reader and my Self. I proceed to the greatest of his Friends situated in high Places: He was very much in favour with the King, and the Duke of *York*, before he declared himself of the Romish Perswasion, whom he Treated magnificently at *Salisbury*. and also with the Archbishop of *Canterbury*, who used to entertain him with the greatest kindness and familiarity imaginable; in his common discourse to him, he used to call him *Old Sarum*: And I have heard the Archbishop speak of him more than once, as the Person whom he wished might succeed him.

About this time, as it is notoriously known, there were Intrigues carried on by a Party at Court, to introduce the Romish Religi-
on,

on, and make the Power of the King Un-
limited, and Arbitrary, whereunto all Persons were to obey without reserve; which
words were in one of the Proclamations
sent to *Scotland*. But the Bishop of *Salisbury* not swimming with the Stream, he lost
at least one of his great Friends, and with
him his favour at Court; the Effects whereof appeared not long after, the manner thus.

The Revenue belonging to the Order of
the Garter, was usually received by the
Chancellor, and he paid the Officers and
the poor Knights of *Windsor*, the Surplus
the King had formerly granted to Sir *Henry
de Vic*, and it was quietly possest by him
till he died, out of which he was to defray
the Charges and Fees of Admission of fo-
reign Princes and Noblemen who were
elected into that Order: For this also, the
Bishop of *Salisbury* had the Kings Hand,
which Grant had been firm and irrevocable,
had the Bishop Seald it with the Seal of
the Order, which he kept in his possession,
or causd it to pass the usual Offices, which
had been easie for him to have done then,
being in much favour at Court. But he
made use of neither of these Corroborati-
ons, and afterwards smarted for it sufficiently.

ently. In the last Year of the Reign of
King *Charles* the Second, and the first of
the precipitous decay of the Bishop of *Salisburys* Intellectuals, some sagacious Cour-
tier found out a Flaw in this Grant; whereupon the Bishop was sent for up to *London*,
and obliged to refund the uttermost peny,
which in so many Years amounted to a
considerable Sum, all which his Majesty
took, without any scruple or remorse.

CHAP. XV.

Concerning my Self.

YOU may remember, at the beginning
of the last Chapter, I threatned to
treat at large, of two or three of the Bishops second rate Friends; and here, as the
Saying is, I will make bold to Christen
mine own Child first, for Charity begins
at home, and take this opportunity to put
in my claim to that glorious Title. I say
therefore, and proclaim it to the World,
that I was his hearty, intimate, and unfeigned Friend; I doubt not but that this
proud Assertion will provoke some testy
old-

old-fashion Filosofer, to take me up severely, that such an inconsiderable Fellow as I, should presume to stile my self a Friend to so great a Prelate, since it is evident out of *Aristotle*, that *Amicitia est inter pares, Where there is no Equality there can be no Friendship.* But, I pray you Sir, have a little patience, and hear how I defend my self against *Ipse-dixit*, I will make use of the Shield of *Horace*, who lived in a greater Court, and may be presumd to understand good Manners as well as *Aristotle*, and I make no doubt, but that he had as much Wit too. This I rather believe, because he did not think fit to trouble the World with *entele-cheias*, *entities* and *quiddities*, and such other abstruse unintelligible Metafysical Notions. I say, this *Horace* uses the word *Friend* reciprocally betwixt *Mecenas* and himself; *Quod te sortitus Amicum.* i.e. *That you are my Friend.* And in another place, *Jubesque esse in Amicorum numero.* That is, *You have orderd me to be registerd amongst your Friends.* Nay, he goes yet farther, and boldly averrs, that he deservd to be so, and that, whoever doubted of it, must esteem *Mecenas* a Fool, and not able to choose a worthy Friend, when he took so much care and caution about

about it. *Presertim cautus dignos assumere.*
That is, *You do not choose your Friends hastily and hand over head.* But I shall not bear
pace with *Horace* so far, I only assert, that
there was not a greater inequality betwixt
the Bishop of *Salisbury* and Me, than betwixt *Mecenas* and *Horace.* Our Poet was
meanly descended, and Poor, *Mecenas* had
the *Etrurian* Kings Blood in his Veins, and
was immensly Rich, and, what is yet greater,
chief Favourite to *Augustus,* the most happy and glorious of all the Roman Empe-
rours, and Governour of *Rome,* the Queen
of Cities, and at that time, the greatest and
richest Town in the known World. Having thus made the way plain, I hope I
may say without contradiction, that I was
the Bishop of *Salisburys* Friend, and he was
mine. But some may yet object, how will
you make this appear? Have a little patience, and read on. I did him all the Ser-
vices in my power, I sufferd *Cold* with him
upon *Salisbury* Plains, and *Heat* in his
Chamber where there was always a great
Fire, tho he did not use to sit by it; I
made it my business to delight him, and
divert his Melancholy, nay I may truly say,
I profited him too. I presented him with

an

an excellent Pad Nag, in whom he took much delight, not permitting any one to ride him besides himself, and valued him so highly, that he refusd fifty five Guineas, which Mr. *Baptist May*, Privy Purse to King *Charles* the Second profferd for him; but this Nag afterwards unfortunately died, by a tread upon one of his hinder Heels, notwithstanding the joint endeavours of the best Farriers to cure him: But I forget my self, I am writing the History of Horses. This Nag was given me by my honoured Friend *Charles* Lord *Clifford*, whose kindness I can never enouf acknowledge, and whose death I can never sufficiently lament. I presented him also with some curious Books which I had collected in my Travels, and I taught him *French* and *Italian*, and went through several Treatises with him in those Languages. I read to him frequently, till my Eyes, by a vehement Inflammation, were useless to me, and renderd me less serviceable to him, for above a Years time. This Malady was perfectly curd, by Gods blessing upon Dr. *Turberviles* application, as I have gratefully acknowledged in the eighteenth and nineteenth *Stanzas* of the First Part of the *Salisbury Canto*. I hope therefore,

fore, twill not be thought that the Bishops kindness to me was wholly undeservd, for *Amor, ut Pila, vices exigit.* That is, *Love, like a Ball or a Shuttle-cock, must be returnd, and held up on both sides.* I acknowledge he was very kind and obliging to me, but yet I would not have the Reader run away with an opinion, that he heapd mountains of Gold upon me; I had, I acknowledge, my Diet and Lodging with him as long and as often as I pleasd; and when we Traveld together, or to speak with more respect, when I accompanied him or attended him in any Journey, he defrayd my Charges, as one of his Retinue. Besides this, I never received of him, directly or indirectly, in Money, or Moneys-worth, to the value of Ten Pounds; and after his death, my Name was not so much as mentioned in the Will, and it cannot be imagind that I expect any Reward for writing his Life now, so many Years after he has been bereavd of it; tho' I confess he did, more than once, proffer me Money when I was Sick in *London.* To what I said before, that his Favours were not wholly undeservd, I will take the boldness to add

here,

here, neither were they wholly cast away, for they fell into good Ground, and have produced a Gratitude in me, which lives, and encreases still, tho' he is dead. 'Tis not every one that will continue his Devotions and Thanks-Offerings, when the Altar is turnd to Dust, and the Saint removd. He did as great and greater Favours to many others, which puts me in mind of that Saying in the Gospel, *Nonne Decem facti sunt mundi? Sed ubi sunt novem?* That is, *Were there not Ten cleansed? but what's become of Nine of them?* not any returning Thanks besides this one. There are yet two other good Friends of the Bishops, and mine also, who must not be passd over in silence; Persons of that Eminency for Learning, Piety, and Vertue, that I never thought my self worthy to unloose their Shoo-latchets, tho' they did not make that figure in the World, as those great ones mentiond in the last Chapter. These were Mr. *Laurence Rooke*, Professor of Geometry in *Gresham-College*, and Dr. *Isaac Barrow*, of whom we shall treat in order, in the ensuing Chapters, only begging leave for a small digression between, concerning Dr. *Turbervile*.

CHAP.

CHAP. XVI.

Of Doctor Turbervile.

HAving casually mentioned Dr. *Turbervile* in the precedent Chapter, I should esteem my self unpardonable, as guilty of the greatest Ingratitude, to dismiss him in so few words; *him*, to whom, under God, I owe my Sight, a blessing, in my opinion, equal, if not preferable, to Life it self, without it. It was he, who twice rescued me from Blindness, which without his aid, had been unavoidable, when both my Eyes were so bad, that with the best I could not perceive a Letter in a Book, nor my Hand with the other, and grew worse and worse every day. Therefore, tho I might treat of him as a Friend to the Bishop, I chose rather to introduce him as mine, because I was more intimately acquainted with him, and as it appears, by what has been said before, infinitely obliged to him.

Dr. *Turbervile* was born at *Wayford*, in *Somerset-shire, Anno. Dom.* 1612, of an ancient

ent Equestrian Family, there being in the Church of *Beer* only, the Tombs of no less than fifteen Knights of that Name, as I am credibly informd, for I confess I have not seen them. By his Mothers side he was Nobly extracted from the Family of the *Dawbignies*, which has afforded this Kingdom many Peers; this Name did his Mothers Father, who was also his Godfather, give him when he was Baptized. Upon his going to the University, his Mother advisd him to make the Diseases of the Eyes his principal study, assuring him, he would find it turn to a good account. He was admitted in *Oriel College* in *Oxford*, and there took the Degree of Dr. of Fysic. When the Civil Wars broke out, he left the University, and bore Arms in defence of the King, Church, and the Establisht Laws; he was in *Exeter* when it was besiegd, and till it was surrendred to the Parliament Forces. Whilst he was shut up therein, he and his Comrade run in Debt a hundred pounds each, in Chalk behind the Door; he told me, that his Landlord came into their Chamber, leading his Daughter by the hand, and courteously profferd to Cancel the Debts of either of them who should

Marry

Marry her: The Dr. valiantly resisted this Temptation, and chose rather to pay his Debts in ready Money, which he did shortly after; the other accepted the Terms, and had his Wifes Portion presently paid him; *viz. His Scores wiped out with a wet Dishclout.*

By the Articles, the Garison might return to their Dwellings, and live there unmolested; he accordingly went to *Wayford*, and Married his only Wife, by whom he had no Children, and who died a few Months before him. At his own House, and at *Crookhorn*, the next adjacent Market-Town, he practisd some time, but finding those Places not capable to entertain the multitude that resorted to him, he removd to *London*, with an intent to reside there; but the Air of that City not agreeing with his Constitution, he left it, and fixd his abode in *Salisbury*, whence he made several Journeys to *London*, either upon his own occasion, or calld thither by some Persons of Quality, wanting his Advice. Once he was sent for by the Dutchess of *York*, to Cure the Princess of *Denmark*, then a Child, labouring under a dangerous Inflammation in her Eyes, and a breaking out

in

K

in her Face, the Cure of which had been attempted in vain by the Court Fysicians. These despisd Dr. *Turbervile*, looking on him as a Country Quack, and demanded what Method he would use, and to see, approve, or reject his Medicaments, before he applyd them, which he refusd, telling her Royal Highness, that if she pleasd to commit her Daughter to his sole management, he would use his utmost endeavour to Cure her, but he would have nothing to do with the Fysicians. He told me, he expected to learn something of those Court Doctors, but, to his amazement, he found them only Spies upon his Practice, and wholly ignorant as to the Ladys Case; nay farther, that he knew several Midwives and Old Women, whose Advice he would rather follow than theirs. The Dutchess yielded, the Surgeons and Fysicians were dismissd, and he alone intrusted with the Lady, whom, to his great reputation and some profit, in few months, fewer than could be expected, he perfectly cured of both those Distempers. I said *some profit*, for tho the Duke orderd him six hundred pound, he could never receive more than half of it; which, considering the Quality of the Patient,

ent, the Expence of the Doctors Journey to and from *London*, and for Lodging, and Diet there, his long attendance at Court, and neglecting other Patients, cannot be esteemd a competent Gratuity.

Many Years after he was calld up again, by one of the greatest and ancientest Peers of this Kingdom, to whom, after having attentively inspected his Eye, he spoke after this manner; *My Lord, I might bear you in hand*, a Western Frase, signifying to delay or keep in expectation, *and feed you with promises, or at least hopes, that I should Cure you in some competent time, and so cause your Lordship to be at great expence to no purpose*; *I cannot Cure you, and I believe no Man in* England *can*. The Earl answerd, *Such and such will undertake it for a hundred pound.* To which the Dr. replied, *I have so great an Honour for your Lordship, and so much wish your Welfare, that I will joyfully give a hundred Guineas out of my own Purse, to the Person who shall restore your Sight in that Eye. I confess I am not able to Cure it, but I can reduce it to a better figure.* Thus they parted; this Nobleman is living, and in a very Eminent Station at my writing this, but has not recoverd that Eye, nor is in any hopes

of

of it, being long since convincd it is incurable.

Dr. *Turbervile* was no boaster, nor would he promise to Cure any Distemper; but when Patients came, he would first look into their Eyes, then tell them their Diseases, and his opinion concerning them; to some he would say, you're Incurable, and would not meddle with them; to others, that he had often Cured such a Malady, and sometimes faild of it, but if they would make use of him, he would do his best.

He generally prescribd to all, shaving their Heads and taking Tobacco, which he had often known to do much good, and never any harm to the Eyes. He did not rely upon two or three Waters or Powders, as most do, for he throughly understood all the Simples and Ingredients, conducing to the Cure of Eyes, compounding Medicaments out of them, with the manner and season of applying them. He has often said to me, during my long being under his hand, after inspecting my Eyes, *I know what to give you now, but cannot tell what I shall to morrow; this Water would make others blind, but your Eyes will bear it*. Hence it follows, that it is at best, but by Chance, if such

Maladies

Maladies are cured at a distance, I mean, when the diseased are so far removd from the Artist, that he cannot visit them often, and observe the Operation of his Medicaments.

I have said before, that the Doctor was Loyal, I will add, he was also a Pious Man, and a good Christian, that he constantly frequented the Public Prayers, and Sermons, and often receivd the Holy Sacrament with exemplary Piety and Devotion.

Add to this; He was far from being Covetous; he Curd the Poor *Gratis*, and receivd from others what they pleasd to give him; never, that I knew, making any Bargain for *so much in hand, and the rest when the Cure is perfected*, as some do. I could not force any thing upon him, for his Medicines and extraordinary Care, unless it were a Cane, a Tobacco-Box, or some new Book, tho I was indebted to him for all the Comforts of my Life.

He has curd several who were born blind, but I do not look upon that as so great a thing; for the cure of such, if curable, for there are several sorts of Cataracts uncurable, consists wholly in this; *viz. In knowing when the connate Cataract is fit to be Couchd,*

Couchd, in having a steady Hand, and skill to perform that Operation, to be able to prevent or at least, remove the pains which usually follow, and sometimes kill the Patient: But *to reduce fallen and inverted Eye-lids to their proper place and Tone, to cure inveterate Ulcers, and Inflammations of a blackish colour, requires a consummate Artist. Hic Labor, hoc opus est.*

To proceed; his Fame brought multitudes to him, from all parts of this and the neighbouring Kingdoms, and even from *America*, whereof take this Instance: I met casually a Friend upon the *Exchange*, who told me, as he was walking upon *Tower-Wharf* that morning, he saw a young Woman coming out of a Boat, who as soon as she had set foot on Land, kneeld down and said these words, which he being near overheard. *Oh Lord God, I pray thee, that I may find Dr.* Turbervile *living, and not make this long Voyage in vain.* To whom he replied, *Madam, be of good comfort, he is alive, and in good health, I have receivd a Letter from him very lately. Your News,* she answerd, *is more acceptable to me than if you had given me a thousand pounds.* What follows I had from the Doctors own mouth:
She

She went to *Salisbury*, and by Gods blessing on the Doctors endeavours, was perfectly cured; but her Joy did not last long, for in her return to *Jamaica*, of which Island her Husband was one of the principal Inhabitants, she died of the Small-Pox in *London*.

This Concourse forementioned, was very beneficial to the Inns and private Houses in *Salisbury*, being dispersd thro' all the quarters of the City, insomuch, that one could scarce peep out of doors, but he had a prospect of some led by Boys, or Women, others with Bandages over one, or both Eyes, and yet a greater number wearing green Silk upon their Faces, which if a Stranger should see, without knowing the reason of that Fenomenon, I should not wonder, if he believd and reported the Air of *Salisbury* to be as pernicious to the *Eyes* as that of *Orleans* is to the *Nerves*, where almost one third of the Inhabitants are Lame. The Rendevouz of these Hoodwinkt People was at the Doctors House, whither I frequently resorted, either to be dressd my self, or see others: I saw many remarkable Passages, whereof I shall relate but two.

The

The first is of a Country-man, whose Eye was Blood-shot, who spoke thus to the Doctor: *I am a little troubled with a sore Eye, which I am come to thee to mend. Which Eye is it,* said the Doctor? *This,* he replyed, pointing to it. The Doctor answerd, *That is your best Eye. I see as well with that,* replied the Country Fellow, *as thee dost, or any Man in* England. Whereupon the Doctor claps his Hand before that Eye he complaind of, and askd, *What see you now?* At which he cried out, *I see nothing, I am blind*; tho to all the rest who were there, that seemed a good Eye.

The other is of such another Person who came to the Doctor upon the like account; his Eye was Protuberant and could not be containd within the Lids, and seemd like a piece of raw Flesh; the Doctor placd him in a Chair, and with a pair of Scissors cut large Gobbets, the blood trickling down his Cheeks in abundance, and yet he seemd no more concernd, than if it had been a Barber cutting his Hair: I was surprizd at his behaviour, and said to one of the bystanders, *Without doubt, this is a Married Man, otherwise 'twere impossible he should be so patient*: Which he over-hearing, in the midst

midst of his Torment, burst out into a loud laughter, and replied, *No indeed, I am but a Batchelor.*

To conclude this long Chapter, Dr. *Turbervile* died at *Salisbury* the 21*st.* of *April,* in the Year of our Lord, 1696, and of his Age the 85*th.* and left a considerable Estate in Money, betwixt a Neice of his Wifes, and his Sister Mrs. *Mary Turbervile,* who now practises in *London* with good Reputation and Success: She has all her Brothers Receipts, and having seen his Practise during many Years, knows how to use them. For my part, I have so good an opinion of her Skill, that should I again be afflicted with sore Eyes, which God forbid, I would rely upon her Advice, rather than upon any Pretenders or Professors in *London,* or elsewhere. He is Buried in the Cathedral Church in *Salisbury.*

ADIEU my dear Friend, à rivederci, till we meet and see one another again, with Eyes which will never stand in need of a COLLYRIUM.

His

His E P I T A F.

M. S.

NEar this Place, lies Interrd the most Expert, and Successful Oculist that ever was, perhaps that ever will be, 𝔇𝔬𝔠𝔱𝔬𝔯 𝔇𝔞𝔴𝔟𝔦𝔤𝔫𝔶 𝔗𝔲𝔯𝔟𝔢𝔯𝔳𝔦𝔩𝔢, *Descended from two Families of those Names, than which, there are few more Ancient and Noble. During the Civil Wars, he bore Arms for the King. After the Surrender of* Exeter, *he livd at* Wayford, *and* Crookhorn; *but those Towns not affording Convenience to his numerous Patients, he removd to* London, *intending to settle there, but not having his health, he left it, and livd in* Salisbury *more than Thirty Years, doing Good to all, and being belovd by all. His great Fame causd multitudes to flock to him, not only from all parts of this Kingdom, but also from* Scotland, Ireland, France, *and* America. *He died April* 21st. 1696, *in the* 85th. *Year of his Age. And left his Estate betwixt his only Sister and Neice, at whose Expences this Monument was Erected.*

Doctor WALTER POPE *wrote this Epitaf, to perpetuate his Gratitude, and the Memory of his Friend and Benefactor.*

CHAP.

CHAP. XVII.

Of Mr. ROOKE.

MR. *Laurence Rooke* was born in *Kent*, of a good Family, and educated in *Cambridge*, and when Dr. *Ward* was transplanted to *Oxford*, he came thither, and seated himself in *Wadham-College*, for the benefit of his Conversation, bringing with him two young Gentlemen of the Family of *Oxenborogh*, to whom he was Tutor. He was very eminent in the famous Filosofical Meeting, which was after turnd into the Royal Society. After the Kings Return, he left *Oxford*, and repair'd to *London*, with his Friend Dr. *Ward*, and was chosen, first Professor of Astronomy, and afterwards of Geometry, in *Gresham-College*. He was also one of the first Members of the Royal Society. He was of a melancholy Temper and Aspect, his Complexion swarthy, his Eyes sunk in his Head more than ordinary, his Voice hoarse and inward, a sign that his Lungs were not sound; he was also much subject to the Scurvy, for which he

usd

usd frequently to take the Juice of Scurvy-grass pressd out of the Leaves without any other Preparation. He was profoundly skilld in all sorts of Learning, not except-ing Botanics and Music, and the abstrusest Points of Divinity. He was my intimate Friend, and in my judgment, the greatest Man in *England* for solid Learning, *Semper excipio Platonem, Tranne Rinaldo*, for Dr. *Barrow* had not then reachd his Zenith. I durst venture my Life upon the Truth of any Proposition he asserted, either in Ma-thematics, Natural Filosofy, or History; for I never knew him affirm any thing positive-ly, that was dubious. I have said to him, Mr. *Rooke*, I have found out the reason of such a Fenomenon, and given him my Argu-ments for it, which when he had heard, he has often replied in this manner; And why may it not as well be thus, bringing his reasons for another Hypothesis. Lord, said I then to him, now you confound me, pray tell me what is your Opinion? To which his usual Answer was, *I have no Opinion*. He was very modest and sparing of his words, unless amongst intimate Friends, and never talkd idly; I may truly say, I never was acquainted with any Person, who

knew

knew more, and spoke less. I usd in all
Company to magnifie and extol his Learning and Ingenuity, as it deservd; insomuch, that an eminent Citizens Wife desird me to help her to a sight of this pro-
digy of Perfection, and to bring him upon
a day appointed, to Dine with her Husband, who was an ingenious Person, and
well known to us both. I prevaild with
him to go, tho' not without some reluctancy.
Thither we went, and found there several
Strangers, whom Madam had invited, like
the Widow in the Gospel, with a *Come,
come Neighbours, and see the Man that is so
Famous.* Amongst the Guests there were
some who valued their selves for their
Wit and Learning, more than they ought;
these towards the latter end of the Dinner,
began to shew their Parts, and fell upon
several Arguments, talking ignorantly, dog-
matically, and ridiculously, which Mr. *Rooke*
heard, I cant say with patience, but without interposing one word. After Dinner,
the Mistress of the House came insultingly to
me, saying, I'll never take your word more
for an Ingenious Man; you saw, how he
let my Friends assert what they pleasd, and
was not able to hold up the Cudgels against
them;

them; nay he did not speak one Quibble, or make one brisk Repartee all Dinner time; is this your magnifyd Wit? Madam, I replied, there's a time for all things; I assure you he can discourse as well as those City Wits your Friends, but I cannot tell you the reason of his silence. Afterwards I askd him why he let those Fools run on at such a rate, when it had been easie for him, with one word, to have convincd them of their ignorance, and put them to silence. I remember he gave me this Answer. *'Tis true, they were a company of positive, ignorant, and self-conceited Fools; if I had interposd, it was a thousand to one, I should not have made them wiser, and as much odds, that I should have made them mine Enemies.* I will make bold with my Self, and here relate a Passage, which equally shews my Folly, and his Wisdom and Sagacity.

When I was a young Student at *Oxford*, I had an old cast Soldier for my Bed-maker, amongst other questions, I askd him where he had servd; he answerd, both in *Flanders* and *France*: Then you speak *French*, I replied: Yes, Master, said he, and very well: What, said I, is *French* for such and such

such a thing? To which when he had answerd, *Will*, said I, you shall be my Master, and teach me *French:* With his help, and some silly Books, I soon thought I had attaind to the mastery of the French Language; and not long after I went to *London*, carrying this opinion of my self with me. Being arrived there, I wished with great impatience, for *Sunday*: *Sunday* came, I repaird early to the French Church in *Thread-Needle-street*: I was very attentive, and staid there a considerable time, but, to my great mortification, I understood not one word the Minister spoke. I was amazd, and considerd how this could be; at last it came into my remembrance, that I had heard, the *French* and *Dutch* did once a Month interchange Churches, which was true, and that it was my misfortune to come upon that Day. This satisfied me, and kept alive my good opinion of my skill in *French*, which this accident had almost destroyd. Upon this I went to Mr. *Rooke*, and declard to him my Adventure; Mr. *Rooke*, said I to him, *you know I understand* French *very well*: *I know*, said he, *that you say so: I'll tell you*, I replied, *a strange Accident that befel me: I went to the French Church*,

Church, and tho I was very attentive for a good while, I came away as ignorant as I enterd the Church, not understanding so much as one word. But at last I found out the reason of it, and contented my self, considering that it might be the turn of the Dutch *to Preach there that* Sunday, *for you know they once a Month change Churches.* 'Tis true, *said he,* it might be so, but answer me one Question; Did the Minister Preach with his Hat on or off? I replied, His Head was covered: Then, *said he,* 'twas a French Sermon; and now I hope you are convincd how well you understand that Language.* This just reproof abated my Pride, and made me entertain a meaner opinion of my Accomplishments, and went a great way towards my Cure, which was afterwards compleated by an Accident which befel me in *France,* and I think I have had no return of that Disease since. Which Story, tho' it makes little to my Credit, take as follows.

In making the Grand Tour of *France,* we lodgd at a Village near *La Rochelle,* whose Name I have forgot; the Travellers were so many, that we were forced to Sup in a Barn, upon several Tables and Forms, there being no room in the Inn capable of

so

so great a Company. The Supper and
Wine was good, and I had taken a chearful Cup, tho not to excess, yet sufficient
to cause me to do that, which otherwise I
should not have done. The Scholars of
Oxford, and I amongst the rest, had a foolish
Frolic when they were in their Merriment,
to twirle round the Hats of those who sate
near them, and call them Cuckolds. This
did I, not considering where, or in what
Company I was, to a French Gentleman
who sate over-against me: upon which he
immediately leaps from his Seat, runs to
me, and kisses me on both Cheeks, adding
these words; *Sir, I am more obliged to you
than to any Person in the World. And why,
Sir?* replied I. *Because*, said he, *you have
pickt me out for so good a naturd Man, that
would not take this action of yours for an
Affront.* I replied, with much shame, *Sir,
you have Cured me, I humbly thank you for it;
had I met with a Person of less discretion, who
could not distinguish betwixt an ignorant Strangers Frolic, and a designd Affront, it might
have endangered my Life, whereas I shall now
only lose an ill Custom, which is better lost than
retaind.*

But to return to Dr. *Rooke*: He had with
great

great Study, and many Observations, almost completed the Theory of the *Satellites* of *Jupiter*; I say almost, for he told me, he wanted but one Observation more, upon such a Night, which happened when he was sick in Bed, and very near his death. He desired me to go to the Society, who were then sitting, and present his Service to them, and acquaint them, that if he had been in Health, to have made an Observation that ensuing Night, he should have compleated the Theory of the *Satellites* of *Jupiter*, but since now it was impossible for him to do it, he desired some others might be employed; but nothing came of it, and his Papers, which he left to the Bishop of *Exeter*, for ought I know, have since perisht. Dr. *Scarboroughs* House was, as I have declared before in the Third Chapter, the Rendezvous of most of the learned Men about *London*, especially of those of the Royal Party, in the Year 1649, but how long before I cannot exactly pronounce, but I guess it must be about three Years, that is from the Surrender of *Oxford*, after the King had made his escape thence in disguise, and retird to the Scotch Army, who then, in conjunction with the English, besieged
Newark,

Newark, Anno Dom. 1646. At which time, Dr. *Scarborough* left *Oxford*, and began to practice in *London*; amongst those who frequented his House, was Mr. *Hobbs*, then newly arrived from *France*, where he had obtained a great reputation for his Book *De Cive*, which is a good Book in the main, and much better than his *Leviathan*; for in the first, there is *Verbum Sapienti*, enouf said, to let the intelligent Reader know what he would be at; but in his *Leviathan* he spreads his Butter so thin, that the courseness of his Bread is plainly perceived under it. This Mr. *Hobbs*, I say, was just come from *Paris*, in order to Print his *Leviathan* at *London*, to curry favour with the Government. He had a good conceit of himself, and was impatient of Contradiction: As he was Older than any of that Convention, he also thought himself Wiser; if any one objected against his Dictates, he would leave the Company in a passion, saying, his business was to Teach, not Dispute. He had entertaind an aversion to Dr. *Ward*, for having written something against him, as we have mentioned in the Fourth Chapter; and before he would enter into the Assembly, he would enquire if Dr. *Ward* was

there,

there, and if he came not in, or if Dr. *Ward* came thither while he was there, Mr. *Hobbs* would immediately leave the Company. So that Dr. *Ward*, tho he much desir'd it, never had any conversation with Mr. *Hobbs*. About this time Mr. *Hobbs* published a little Treatise concerning Mathematics, wherein, amongst other things, he pretends to give the Square of a Circle; which when Mr. *Rooke* read and consider'd, he found it false, and went to Mr. *Hobbs* to acquaint him with it, but he had no patience to hear him; therefore when he went next to visit Mr. *Hobbs*, he carried with him a Confutation of his Quadrature, and left it behind him at his departure. Mr. *Hobbs* finds and reads it, and by want of attention, casts it up wrong, for it was accurately Calculated, and truly written, and thence insultingly concludes, since that Learned Persons Confutation was false, his own Quadrature must of necessity be true. A Year or two before Mr. *Rookes* death, the Marquis of *Dorchester*, who profess'd so great knowledge in almost all sorts of Learning, being a Doctor of Fysic, admitted into the College and practising, a Counsellour at Common Law, and at *Doctors-Commons*, &c.

was

was pleasd to make choice of Mr. *Rooke*
for his Companion, and Fellow-labourer in
Filosofy and Mathematics; the Marquis
lived then at his House at *Highgate*, from
whence every *Wednesday*, he used to bring
Mr. *Rooke* in his Coach to the Royal Society,
then sitting at *Gresham-College*. The last
time Mr. *Rooke* came from thence, he walkd
it, and that so fast, in the heat of Summer,
that he sweat, and caught Cold upon it,
and finding himself much indisposd, lodgd
at his Chamber in the College that Night.
Next morning I went to visit him, and perceived his Countenance much altered, more
than is usual in sick Persons, in so short a
time; he was not very hot, nor was his
Pulse high, his Feaver being Internal and
very Malignant. All the best Fysicians in
London, for they were all his Friends, and
Acquaintance came to see him, and went
away presently, shaking their Heads, and
despairing of his recovery; but yet that
they might seem to do something, they ordered him to Bleed, to be Blisterd, to have
Plaisters applied to his Wrists, and the soles
of his Feet: when the Surgeon came, he
appointed him to open such a Vein, for
under that there lies no Artery; this he
did

did to prevent an *Aneurism*. He made a Nuncupatory Will, leaving what he had to his old Friend Dr. *Ward*, then newly nominated to the Bishopric of *Exeter*; the Bishop Buried him decently, at St. *Martins Outwich*, near *Gresham-College*, and his Corps was attended to the Grave by most of the Fellows of the Royal Society who were then in Town, lamenting theirs, and the Learned Worlds loss. In his Will he ordered that his Executor might receive what was due to him by Bond, if they who were bound did proffer the payment willingly; but *I would not*, said he, *have him Sue the Bonds; for as I never was in Law, or had any Contention with any Man in my life, neither would I be after my death.* In the Memory of his deceased Friend, Bishop *Ward* gave to the Royal Society a large Pendulum Clock, made by *Fromantel*, and then esteemed a great Rarity, and set it up in the Room of their Meeting, upon which were engravd these words:

Societati Regali ad Scientiam Naturalem promovendam institutæ, dono dedit. Reverendus in Christo Pater Sethus Episcopus Exon, ejusdem Societatis Sodalis, in memoriam Laurentii Rooke viri in omni literarum genere instructissimi,

structissimi, Collegii Greshamensis primum As-
tronomiæ deinde Geometriæ Professoris dictæque
Societatis nuper sodalis, Qui obiit Junii 26.
Anno Dom. 1662. That is,

Seth *Bishop of* Exeter, *gave this to the*
Royal Society to be set up in the place of their
Meeting, in Memory of Mr. Lawrence Rooke,
a Person throughly skilld in all sorts of good
Literature; *first, Astronomy, afterwards Geo-*
metry Professor in Gresham-College, *who died*
the 26. *of* June, *in the Year of our Lord*, 1662.
What I have more to say of him, shall be
delivered in the ensuing Chapter.

CHAP. XVIII.

A Continuation of the precedent Chapter.

THey who are desirous to know more
of Mr. *Rooke*, may, if they please,
have recourse to what Dr. *Barrow* says of
him in his Auguration Speech, when he
succeeded him in the Professor of Geome-
trys place in *Gresham-College*. This Oration
is printed in the fourth Volume of Dr. *Bar-*
rows Works; and what concerns Mr. *Rooke*,
begins in the Ninety third Page, towards the
bottom

bottom of it. There they will find a great, and yet a just and true Character of him, as all those who knew him must acknowledge, and that managed with much Art and written with great Eloquence; but what is most remarkable, he begins with an admirable turn of Wit, making use of a Topic to gain Credence with his Auditory, which seems adapted to work the contrary Effect. Before he enters upon his Panegyric, he francly confesses that he did not know Mr. *Rooke*; now one would think, this should strike a damp upon the Auditors, and cause them to reason thus: If this Orator knew not the Person whom he undertakes to praise, what reason have we to believe what he says of him? certainly we have none at all. Which Objection he thus anticipates: Even for that, says he, you ought to give greater Credit to my Words; for had he been my Acquaintance, near Relation, or intimate Friend, I might have been bribd by my Love to him, and suspected to have lookt on him with Magnifying Glasses, and have both perceivd and represented his Vertues greater than they were; but now I am free from any such suspicion, speaking of him only by Hear-say, or Report; but

what

what Report? The constant, universal, and uncontradicted Suffrage of all Learned and Wise Men: But it sounds better in his own Words. *Antecessorum, ut tempore postremus, ita nulli postponendus, vir infelici ne dissimulem mihi, non nisi de longinquo & famæ tantum beneficio cognitas, famæ tamen haud vulgaris aut dubiæ, sed optimorum complurium & prestantissimorum virorum consona autoritate subnixæ quo paratiorem mea verba, non ab effectu privato dictata sed veritatis vi expressa, non Amicitiæ juri debita sed virtutis reverentiæ data, sibi fidem deposcant. Quid enim qui virtutum suarum segniter animos irritanti fama, non admodum credulæ facilitatis homines admiratione perculit, corripuitque amore, qui sibi necdum visos penitasque ignotos studio devinxit sui, & desiderio inflammavit qualem quantumque esse virum oportuit? Tui certe similem, Divine Laurenti, ut potein quo, cum omnigena Scientia rerum, incorrupta Probitas morum, cum intelligentia magis quam virili, plus quam virgi pudor, cum sagacissima prudentia, candidissima simplicitas, cum profunda soliditate judicii perspicax Acumen ingenii, cum vivida alacritate mentis, invicta laboris patientia, cum illibata denique severitate vitæ suæ, suavissima conversandi tenitas, raro quodom,*

quodom, & vix credibili temperamento conspi-
rarint. Non unius, is scilicet aut alterius
Scientiæ tenui rore aspersus, sed omnium fuit
denso imbre perfusus, nec extimam duntaxat
cutem rerum perstrinxit notitiæ, sed abstru-
sissima viscera pervasit, &c. That is,

'He was the last of my Predecessors in
'Time, but in nothing else behind the best
'of them: I must not dissemble my infe-
'licity, in not knowing him but at a di-
'stance, and by report of others; but what
'report? Not a dubious and uncertain
'Rumour, spread abroad by a few, unlearn-
'ed, and inconsiderable Persons, but by a
'constant and uncontradicted Fame, groun-
'ded upon the agreeing Suffrages of all
'the wisest and best Men; my Words
'therefore are more worthy of belief, as
'not proceeding from Affection to him,
'but from the force of Truth, not due to
'Friendship, but offerd to the reverence of
'Virtue: For what manner of Man ought
'he to be? Who could affect Persons not
'credulous, or of an easie Impression,
'with an admiration of him, and inflame
'those with Love to him whom he had
'never seen, and who were perfectly un-
'known to him? It must only be, such a
'one

' one as you, Divine *Laurence*, in whom an
' incorrupt probity of Manners, was joynd
' with an universal knowledge of things, a
' more than Virgin Modesty, with a more
' than Virile Understanding, a most Can-
' did Simplicity, with a most Sagacious
' Prudence, a Perspicatious sharpness of
' Wit, with a profound Solidity of Judg-
' ment, an invincible Patience of Labour,
' with a vivid Chearfulness of Mind, and
' lastly, with a severe unblamable Life, a
' most sweet manner of Conversation; all
' these conspird in thee, by a rare, and al-
' most incredible Temperament. He was
' not lightly sprinkled with the thin Dew
' of one or two Sciences, but throughly
' moistned with plenteous Showers of all;
' He did not content himself with a super-
' ficial skin-deep Knowledge of things, but
' penetrated into their Bowels, and most
' abstruse Recesses, *&c.*

Before the Bishop of *Exeter* resolvd to
give a Pendulum Clock to the Royal Society, to preserve Mr. *Rookes* Memory, he
design'd to have put up an Inscription over
or near the place of his Interrment; for that
end, Dr. *Bathurst*, now Dean of *Wells*,
composd an ingenious Epitaf, very worthy

to

to be here inserted, this was communicated to me by my worthy Friend *Abraham Hill* Esquire, so often before mentioned, 'tis as follows.

M. S.

Hic subtus sive dormit, sive meditatur,
Qui jamdudum animo metitus est,
Quicquid, aut vita, aut mors habet.
V. C. Laurentius Rooke, *è Cantio oriundus*
In Collegio Greshamensi
Astronomiæ primum, dein Geometriæ Professor,
Utriusque Ornamentum & Spes maxima;
Quem altissima Indoles, Artesque omnifariæ,
Mores pellucidi, & ad amussim probi,
Consuetudo facilis, & accommoda,
Bonis, Doctisq; omnibus, fecerunt commenda-
tissimum.
Vir totus teres, & sui plenus,
Cui virtus, & pietas, & summa ratio,
Desideria motusque omnes sub pedibus dabant,
Ne se penitus sæculo subducere mortuus possit,
Qui iniquissima Modestia vixerat,
Sethus Ward *Episcopus* Exon.
Longas, suavesque Amicitias,
Hoc Saxo prosecutus est.
Obiit Junii 27. Anno Dom. MDCLXII.
Ætatis suæ XL.

In

In English thus.

'To the Pious Memory
' Of that Excellent Person, *Laurence Rooke*,
'Who either sleeps, or meditates under this
      Stone,
' Who was born in *Kent*, and successively
      ' Enjoyd the Professors Place of
        ' Astronomy, and Geometry,
            ' In *Gresham-College*,
' Of both those Sciences being Ornament
        ' and greatest Hope.
  ' In his Life-time, he had measurd
          ' and comprehended
  What ever is in Life or Death.
' He was highly esteemd by all good and
          ' Learned Men,
' For the admirable Temper of his Mind,
' Universal Erudition, sweet and transparent
          ' Manners,
' Exact and consummate Vertue, easie and
        ' profitable Conversation,
' Being full of Knowledge, but not puft up.
' By his Piety, Virtue, and exalted Reason,
' He had subdued, and trod under his Feet,
      ' All Worldly Desires, and Fears.
' But lest he, whom a most unjust Modesty
      ' Obscurd so much in his Life,
                          ' Should

' Should be unknown to all after his Death,
　' *Seth Ward*, Bishop of *Exeter*,
' In return for their long and most sweet
　　' Friendship,
' Has endeavour'd to perpetuate his Memory
　　' by this Monument.
' He died *June* the 27. in the Year of our
　' Lord, 1662. in the Fourtieth
　　　' Year of his Age.

Doctor *Barrow* did not only succeed
Mr. *Rooke* in his Place at *Gresham-College*, but
also in his intimate Friendship with Bishop
Ward; and as such, I shall treat of him in
the ensuing Chapter.

CHAP. XIX.

Of Doctor Barrow.

IT is not my design to write Dr. *Barrows*
Life, and if it were, I am not furnished with sufficient Materials for that under-
taking. It is already done, tho with too
much brevity, by a better hand, dedicated
to the Reverend Dr. *Tillotson*, then Dean,
and afterwards Archbishop of *Canterbury*,
　　　　　　　　　　　　　　　　by

by my worthy, learned, and ingenious Friend, *Abraham Hill*, Esq; out of whose Account I shall take what I before was ignorant of, concerning his Birth and Education, before he arrivd to be so Eminent at *Cambridge*, adding thereunto, several particular Accidents which happened during my intimate acquaintance with him, and sometimes going out of the way for a season, to make the Narration more delightful. I may possibly insert some particulars, which will seem trivial, tho in my opinion, the less considerable Words, and Actions, and Circumstances of great Men, amongst whom, he has a just title to be inrolld, are worthy to be transmitted to Posterity.

Mr. *Hill* fixes Dr. *Barrows* Birth in the Month of *October*, *A. D.* 1630. But I hope he will not be offended if I dissent from him, both as to the Year and Month, and produce Reason for so doing; tis this: I have often heard Dr. *Barrow* say, that he was born upon the Twenty-ninth of *February*; and if he said true, it could not be either in *October*, or in 1630, that not being a Leap Year. I would not have asserted this, merely upon the credit of my Memory, had it been any other Day of any other Month,

Month, it being told me so long since, had I not this remarkable Circumstance to confirm it: He used to say, it is in one respect, the best Day in the Year to be born upon, for it afforded me this advantage over my Fellow Collegiates, who used to keep Feasts upon their Birth-day; I was treated by them once every Year, and I entertaind them once in four Years, when *February* had nine and twenty Days.

Dr. *Barrow* was born in *London*, and well descended; his Great Grandfather was *Fillip Barrow*, who published a Method of Fysic, whose Brother *Isaac* was a Doctor of Fysic, and a Benefactor to *Trinity College* in *Cambridge*, as also a Tutor therein to *Robert Cecill* Earl of *Salisbury*, and Lord-Treasurer of *England*. His Grandfather was *Isaac Barrow* Esquire, of *Spiney-Abbey* in *Cambridge-shire*, a Person of a good Estate, and a Justice of Peace during the space of fourty Years. His Fathers Name was *Thomas*, a reputable Citizen of *London*, and Linnen-Draper to King *Charles* the First, to whose Interests he adherd, following him first to *Oxford*, and after his Execrable Murder, he went to his Son *Charles* the Second, then in Exile, there with great patience
expecting

expecting the Kings Restoration, which at last happened, when twas almost despaird of. I remember Mr. *Abraham Cowley*, who also was beyond Sea with the King, told me, at our first coming into *France*, we expected every Post would bring us News of our being recalld; but having been frustrated for so many Years, we could not believe it when the happy News arrivd. This *Thomas* had a Brother whose Name was *Isaac*, afterwards Bishop of St. *Asaf*, whose Consecration Sermon, his Nevew and Namesake our Dr. *Barrow*, preachd at *Westminster-Abbey*. His Mother was *Ann*, Daughter of *William Buggins* Esq; of *North-Cray* in *Kent*. This Genealogy, tho short, has quite tird my patience, it so little concerns him, for it is certainly the least of his Praises, if it be any at all. To be Nobly or Royally extracted, is the gift of blind Fortune; *A Principibus nasci fortuitum est.* This may happen to an ill and ignorant Person, but to be eminently Learned and Pious, cannot be obtaind, without indefatigable Industry, and a sincere love and constant practice of Vertue. He was first put to the *Charterhouse* School, where he made little or no progress, there appearing in him

an

M

an inclination rather to be a Soldier than a Scholar, his chief delight being in Fighting himself, and encouraging his Play-fellows to it; and he was indeed of an undaunted Courage, as we shall make evident in its place. His Father finding no good was to be hopd for there, removd him to *Felstead* in *Essex*, where contrary to his expectation, and even beyond his hopes, his Son on a sudden, became so great a proficient in Learning, and all other praise-worthy Qualifications, that his Master appointed him Tutor to the Lord Viscount *Fairfax*, of *Emely* in *Ireland*, who was then his Scholar. During his stay at *Felstead*, he was admitted into *Peter-House*, of which College his Uncle the Bishop had formerly been a Member. When he was fit for the University he went to *Cambridge*, and was admitted in *Trinity* in *Febr. A. D.* 1645. He was there kindly treated by Dr. *Hill*, whom the Parliament had put in to that Mastership, in the place of Dr. *Comber*, ejected for adhering to the King. This Dr. *Hill*, I say, one day laying his Hand upon young *Isaacs* Head, *Thou art a good Lad*, said he, *tis pity thou art a Cavalier*; and afterwards, when he had made an Oration upon the Gun-powder Treason,

Treason, wherein he had so celebrated the former Times, as to reflect much on the present, some of the Fellows movd for his Expulsion, but the Master silencd them with these word, Barrow *is a better Man than any of us.* This is very remarkable, and an evident Testimony of our young Scholars irresistible Merits, which could, as the Poets feign of *Orfeus,——Lenire Tigres rapidesque Leones*; that is, *Tame Savage Tigers and fierce Lions*, make a Presbyterian kind to a Cavalier, and Malignant, which Names the adherers to the King, Church, and Laws went under in those days. *Anno Domini* 1649. He was chosen Fellow of the College, carrying it merely by the dint of his Merits, having no Friend to commend him, as being of a contrary Perswasion to those who then carried all things in that University. This brings to my Memory, a Certificate or Testimonial, which my worthy Friend Dr. *Gilbert Ironside*, then Warden of *Wadham-College* in *Oxford*, and now Bishop of *Hereford*, gave to a Member of that College, who was Candidate for a Fellowship in another College, it was to this purpose. *If this Person, whom I recommend to you, be not a better Scholar than any of those who are*

his

his Competitors, choose him not; and he did upon Examination and Trial so far surpass the rest, that they could not refuse him, without being, and appearing Partial, and unjust. I mention this as a Parallel to Dr. *Barrows* Case.

When Doctor *Duport* resignd his Greek Lecture, he recommended his Pupil Mr. *Barrow* for his Successor, who justified his opinion of his fitness for that Employment, by an excellent performance of the Probation Exercise; but the governing Party thinking him inclind to *Arminianism*, put him by it. This disappointment, the melancholy aspect of Public Affairs, together with a desire to see some of those places mentioned in Greek and Latin Writers, made him resolve to Travel; which, that he might be better inabled to do, he converted his Books into ready Money. He began his Travels, *Anno Dom.* 1654, and went first to *Paris*, to crave his Fathers Benediction, who was then in the English Court praying for, but scarce hoping, much less expecting the Kings Restoration, to whom, his pious Son, out of his small Stock, made a seasonable Present. After some Months stay there, he went to *Italy*, and remained
some

some time at that most beautiful City of
Florence, where he had the favour, and neg-
lected it not, to peruse many Books in the
Grand Dukes Library, and ten thousand
curious Medals, and to discourse concerning
them with Mr. *Fitton*, who found his ability so great in that sort of Learning, that
upon his recommendation, the Grand Duke
invited Dr. *Barrow* to take upon him the
Charge and Custody of that great Treasure
of Antiquity. From *Florence* he went to
Leghorne, Anno Dom.   where he was
much Caressd by the English Merchants re-
siding there: Thence he saild to *Smyrna*,
where he met with the like kindness and
entertainment from Consul *Breton*, and the
rest of that Factory: As he did also afterwards at *Constantinople*, from Sir *Thomas
Bendish* the English Ambassador at the *Ot-
toman* Court, Sir *Jonathan Dawes*, and the
rest of the English Merchants, from whom
he received many Favours, and with whom
he ever after continued an intimate Friendship. At *Constantinople* the See of St. *Chry-
sostom*, he read all the Works of that Father,
whom he much preferrd before the rest.
He remained in *Turkey* more than a Year,
and then returnd to *Venice*, where he was

no

no sooner Landed, but the Ship which brought him took Fire, and was, with all its Cargo, consum'd to Ashes, the Men only sav'd. From *Venice*, in his way to *England*, he pass'd by through *Germany* and *Holland*, and has left a Description of some parts of those Countries in his Poems.

Anno Dom. 1660, He was chosen without a Competitor, Professor of the Greek Tongue in *Cambridge*; two Years after, he was elected Professor of Geometry at *Gresham-College*, in the place of Mr. *Laurence Rooke*, concerning whom, we have discours'd at large in the two preceding Chapters.

Anno Dom. 1669, Mr. *Lucas* Founded, and richly endow'd a Mathematical Lecture in *Cambridge*, which his Executors, Mr. *Raworth* and Mr. *Buck*, conferr'd upon Dr. *Barrow*, enjoyning him to leave every Year Ten Lectures in Writing to the University, the better to secure the End of so Noble and Useful a Foundation. The Lectures which are printed, and others of his, ready for the Press, will give the best Account how he behav'd himself in that Employment. Almost all I have hitherto said, is, I acknowledge, taken out of Mr. *Hills* Account of Dr. *Barrows* Life; but now I am got within

within mine own knowledge, and can proceed securely without his Clue, or the help of any other Guide. I promise, I will advance nothing, but what I have good Authority for, but what I have either known my self to be true, or heard from Dr. *Barrows* mouth.

I am not unmindful of my promise, to make it appear in its due place, that Dr. *Barrow* was endued with an undaunted Courage; to prove which, I think these two Instances following will be sufficient. In his passage from *Leghorn* to *Constantinople*, the Ship he saild in was attackd by an *Algerine* Pyrate; during the Fight, he betook himself to his Arms, staid upon the Deck, chearfully and vigorously fighting, till the Pyrate perceiving the stout defence the Ship made, steerd off and left her. I askd him, why he did not go down into the Hold, and leave the defence of the Ship to those to whom it did belong: He replied, It concernd no Man more than my self; I would rather have lost my Life, than have faln into the hands of these merciless Infidels. This Engagement, and his own stout and intrepid behaviour in it, to defend his Liberty, which he valued more than his Life

as

as he asserts in that Verse, *Almaque libertas vitali charior Aura*, he describes at large, in a Copy of Verses in the Fourth Volume of his Works, Printed by *Brabazon Aylmer*. To this I will add another Accident, which befel him in *England*, it being of the like nature: He was at a Gentlemans House in the Country, if I mistake not in *Cambridgeshire*, where the Necessary House was at the end of a long Garden, and consequently at a great distance from the Room where he lodgd, as he was going to it very early, even before Day, for, as I shall shew hereafter, he was sparing of sleep, and an early riser, a fierce Mastiff, who used to be chaind up all Day, and let loose late at Night for the security of the House, perceiving a strange Person in the Garden at that unseasonable time, set upon him with great fury. The Dr catchd him by the Throat, threw him, and lay upon him, and whilst he kept him down, considered what he should do in that Exigent; once he had a mind to kill him, but he quite alterd this resolution, judging it would be an unjust Action, for the Dog did his duty, and he himself was in fault for rambling out of his Lodgings before twas light. At length he calld

calld out so loud, that he was heard by some of the House, who came presently out, and freed both the Doctor and the Dog, from the eminent danger they were both in.

Anno Dom. 1672, Upon the death of Bishop *Wilkins*, Dr. *Pearson*, Master of *Trinity College* in *Cambridge*, was promoted to the Bishopric of *Chester*, and the vacant Mastership was, by the King, conferrd upon Dr. *Barrow*. I will leave him possest of that Post, and look a little backward, and declare some Accidents of his Life, which happened before he had arrivd to that eminent Dignity; but because this Chapter is long enouf already, for the Readers sake and mine own, I will here make a Halt, reserving what remains, to the following Chapters.

CHAP. XX.

The same Matter continued.

AS soon as Dr. *Ward* was made Bishop of *Exeter*, he procured for his old Friend Mr. *Wilkins*, the Rectory of St. *Laurence-Jewry*, who was then destitute of any Place, the reason whereof I have given before:

fore: He being Minister there, and forcd by some Indisposition to keep his Chamber, desird Dr. *Barrow* to give him a Sermon the next *Sunday*, which he readily consented to do. Accordingly, at the time appointed, he came, with an Aspect pale and meagre, and unpromising, slovenly and carelessly dressed, his Collar unbuttond, his Hair uncombd, &c. Thus accoutred, he mounts the Pulpit, begins his Prayer, which, whether he did Read or not, I cannot positively assert, or deny: Immediately all the Congregation was in an uproar, as if the Church were falling, and they scampering to save their Lives, each shifting for himself with great precipitation; there was such a noise of Pattens of Serving-Maids, and ordinary Women, and of unlocking of Pewes, and cracking of Seats, causd by the younger sort hastily climbing over them, that I confess, I thought all the Congregation were mad: But the good Doctor seeming not to take notice of this disturbance, proceeds, names his Text, and preachd his Sermon, to two or three gathered, or rather left together, of which number, as it fortunately happened, Mr. *Baxter*, that Eminent Non-conformist was one, who afterwards

wards gave Dr. *Wilkins* a Visit, and commended the Sermon to that degree, that he said, he never heard a better Discourse: There was also amongst those who staid out the Sermon, a certain young Man, who thus accosted Dr. *Barrow* as he came down from the Pulpit; *Sir, be not dismayd, for I assure you, twas a good Sermon.* By his Age and dress, he seemed to be an Apprentice, or at the best, a Fore-man of a Shop, but we never heard more of him. I askd the Doctor, what he thought, when he saw the Congregation running away from him? *I thought,* said he, *they did not like me, or my Sermon, and I have no reason to be angry with them for that. But what was your opinion,* said I, *of the Apprentice? I take him,* replied he, *to be a very Civil Person, and if I could meet with him I'd present him with a bottle of Wine.* There were then in that Parish a company of formal, grave, and wealthy Citizens, who having been many Years under famous Ministers, as Dr. *Wilkins*, Bishop *Ward*, Bishop *Reynolds*, Mr. *Vines*, &c. had a great opinion of their skill in Divinity, and their ability to judge of the goodness and badness of Sermons: Many of these came in a body to Dr. *Wilkins*,

kins, to expostulate with him, why he sufferd such an Ignorant, Scandalous Fellow, meaning Dr. *Barrow*, to have the use of his Pulpit. I cannot precisely tell, whether it was the same day, or sometime after in that Week, but I am certain it happened to be when Mr. *Baxter* was with Dr. *Wilkins*. They came, as I said before, in full Cry, saying, they wondered he should permit such a Man to Preach before them, who lookt like a starvd Cavalier who had been long Sequesterd, and out of his Living for Delinquency, and came up to *London* to beg, now the King was restord; and much more to this purpose. He let them run their selves out of breath, when they had done speaking, and expected an humble submissive Answer, he replied to them in this manner: *The Person you thus despise, I assure you, is a Pious Man, an Eminent Scholar, and an Excellent Preacher: For the truth of the last, I appeal to Mr.* Baxter *here present, who heard the Sermon, you so vilifie: I am sure you believe Mr.* Baxter *is a competent Judge, and will pronounce according to Truth;* then turning to him, *Pray Sir,* said he, *do me the favour to declare your Opinion concerning the Sermon now in Controversie, which*

you

you heard at our Church the last Sunday. Then did Mr. *Baxter* very candidly give the Sermon the praise it deservd, nay more, he said, *That Dr.* Barrow *Preachd so well, that he could willingly have been his Auditor all day long.* When they heard Mr. *Baxter* give him this high *Encomium,* they were prickt in their hearts, and all of them became a-shamd, confounded, and speechless; for, tho they had a good opinion of their selves, yet they durst not pretend to be equal to Mr. *Baxter*; but at length, after some pause, they all, one after another, confessd, *they did not hear one word of the Sermon, but were carried to mislike it, by his unpromising Garb, and Mien, the Reading of his Prayer, and the going away of the Congregation; for they* would not by any means have it thought, if they had heard the Sermon, they should not have concurrd with the Judgment of Mr. *Baxter.* After their shame was a little over, they earnestly desird Dr. *Wilkins* to procure Dr. *Barrow* to Preach again, enga-ging their selves to make him amends, *by bringing to his Sermon their Wives and Chil-dren, Man-servants, and Maid-servants, in a word, their whole Familes, and to enjoyn them not to leave the Church till the Blessing was pronouncd.*

pronouncd. Dr. *Wilkins* promised them to use his utmost endeavour for their satisfaction, and accordingly solicited Dr. *Barrow* to appear once more upon that Stage, but all in vain, for he would not by any perswasions be prevaild upon to comply with the Request of such conceited, hypocritical Coxcombs. Some time after, the Bishop of *Salisbury*, I mean Dr. *Ward*, invited Dr. *Barrow* to live with him, not as a Chaplain, but rather as a Friend and Companion, yet he did frequently do the duty if the domestic Chaplain was absent. Whilst he was there, the Arch-deaconry of *North-Wiltshire* became void, by the death of Dr. *Childerey*, if I mistake not; this the Bishop profferd Dr. *Barrow*; but he modestly and absolutely refused it, and told me the reason, which it is not necessary I should declare. Not long after a Prebendary died, whose Corps, I mean Revenue, lay in *Dorsetshire*, this also the Bishop offerd him, and he gratefully accepted it, and was Installd accordingly. I remember about that time, I heard him once say, *I wish I had five hundred pounds*. I replied, *Thats a great Sum for a Filosofer to desire, what would you do with so much? I would*, said he, *give it my Sister*

Sister for a Portion, that would procure her a good Husband: Which Sum, in few Months after he received, for putting a Life into the Corps of his new Prebend; after which he resignd it to Mr. *Corker*, a Fellow of *Trinity College* in *Cambridge*. All the While he continued with the Bishop of *Salisbury* I was his Bedfellow, and a witness of his indefatigable Study; at that time he applied himself wholly to Divinity, having given a divorce to Mathematics, and Poetry, and the rest of the *Belles lettres*, wherein he was profoundly versd, making it his chief, if not only business, to write in defence of the Church of *England*, and compose Sermons, whereof he had great store, and, I need not say, very good.

We were once going from *Salisbury* to *London*, he in the Coach with the Bishop, and I on Horseback; as he was entring the Coach, I perceivd his Pockets strutting out near half a Foot, and said to him, *What have you got in your Pockets?* He replied, *Sermons. Sermons*, said I, *give them me, my Boy shall carry them in his Portmanteau, and ease you of that luggage. But*, said he, *suppose your Boy should be robbd: Thats pleasant*, said

said I, *do you think there are Parsons Padding upon the Road for Sermons? Why, what have you*, said he, *it may be five or six Guineas, I hold my Sermons at a greater rate, they cost me much pain and time. Well then*, said I, *if you'll insure my five or six Guineas against Lay-Padders, I'll secure your bundle of Sermons against Ecclesiastical Highway-men*. This was agreed, he emptied his Pockets, and filled my Portmanteau with Divinity, and we had the good fortune to come safe to our Journeys end, without meeting either sort of the Padders forementioned, and to bring both our Treasures to *London*. He was of a healthy Constitution, used no Exercise, or Fysic, besides smoking Tobacco, in which he was not sparing, saying, it was an *instar omnium*, or *panfarmicon*: He was unmercifully cruel to a lean Carcass, not allowing it sufficient Meat or Sleep: during the Winter Months, and some part of the rest, he rose always before it was light, being never without a Tinder-Box and other proper Utensils for that purpose; I have frequently known him, after his first sleep, rise, light, and after burning out his Candle, return to Bed before Day. I say, I have known him do this; I report it not

upon

upon hear-say, but experience, having been, as I said before, his Bedfellow whilst he livd with the Bishop of *Salisbury*. There cannot be a more evident proof of his indefatigability in Study, immense Comprehension, and accurate Attention to what he sought after, than what Mr. *Hill* attests he saw written with his own Hand, at the end of his *Apollonius*. $\frac{\text{April 14.}}{\text{May 10.}}$ *Intra hæc temporis intervalla peractum hoc opus:* That is, *In twenty seven or twenty eight days, this Work was finished:* For there may be five, and must be at least four *Sundays*, whereon I suppose he was otherways employd, betwixt those days. He was careless of his Cloaths, even to a fault; I remember he once made me a Visit, and I perceiving his Band sate very auwkardly, and askd him, *What makes your Band sit so? I have,* said he, *no Buttons upon my Collar. Come,* said I, *put on my Night-Gown, here's a Taylor at hand,* for by chance my Taylor was then with me *who will presently set all things right.* With much ado I prevaild with him; the Buttons were supplied, the Gown made clean, the Hands and Face washt, and the Cloaths and Hat brushd; in a word, at his departure he did not seem the same

Man

N

Man who came in just before. He had one
Fault more, if it deserves that name, he
was generally too long in his Sermons; and
now I have spoken as ill of him as the
worst of his Enemies could, if ever he had
any: He did not consider, that Men cannot be attentive to any Discourse of above
an hours duration, and hardly so long, and
that therefore even in Plays, which are
Discourses made for Diversion, and more
agreeable to Mankind, there are frequent
Pauses and Music betwixt the Acts, that
the Spectators may rise from their Seats and
refresh their weary Bodies and Minds. But
he thought he had not said enouf, if he
omitted any thing that belongd to the subject of his Discourse, so that his Sermons
seemd rather complete Treatises, than O-
rations, designd to be spoke in an hour;
hereof I will give you two or three Instances. He was once requested by the
Bishop of *Rochester* then, and now Dean of
Westminster, to Preach at the Abby, and
withal desird not to be long, for that Auditory lovd short Sermons, and were usd
to them. He replied, My Lord, I will shew
you my Sermon; and pulling it out of his
Pocket, puts it into the Bishops hands. The
Text

Text was in the Tenth Chapter of the *Proverbs*, the latter end of the eighteenth Verse, the words these; *He that uttereth Slander is a Lyer*. The Sermon was accordingly divided into Two Parts, one treated of Slander, the other of Lyes. The Dean desird him to content himself with preaching only the First Part, to which he consented, not without some reluctancy, and in speaking that only, it took up an hour and an half. This Discourse is since published in two Sermons, as it was preachd. Another time, upon the same Persons Invitation, he preachd at the Abby on a Holiday: Here I must inform the Reader, that it is a Custom for the Servants of the Church upon all Holidays, *Sundays* excepted, betwixt the Sermon and Evening Prayers, to shew the Tombs, and Effigies of the Kings and Queens in Wax, to the meaner sort of People, who then flock thither from all the corners of the Town, and pay their Twopence to see *The Play of the Dead Volks*, as I have heard a *Devonshire* Clown not improperly call it. These perceiving Dr. *Barrow* in the Pulpit after the hour was past, and fearing to lose that time in *hearing*, which they thought they could

more

more profitably employ in *receiving*. These, I say, became impatient, and causd the Organ to be struck up against him, and would not give over playing till they had blowd him down. But the Sermon of the greatest length was that concerning Charity, before the Lord Mayor and Aldermen at the *Spittle*; in speaking which, he spent three hours and an half. Being askd, after he came down from the Pulpit, whether he was not tired; *Yes indeed*, said he, *I began to be weary with standing so long.*

Hence I infer, if Dr. *Barrow* thought, as other Men do, which without doubt he did, these Sermons must be of a prodigious length when they came fire-new from the Forge. For every Man who collects Materials for a Building, lays in more than he shall have occasion for. Every Statuary provides more Marble than is necessary to make his Image, much whereof must be cut off with the Chissel, before any proportion or design of the Workman can appear. Every Carpenter makes some Chips, and he is the best Workman who makes fewest, in bringing the Timber to the Figure he designs. It is very easie to make

a

a long Discourse, or a prolix Letter, but to contract it, to remove the Rubbish, to amputate the needless Branches, which keep out the Light, and bear no Fruit; in a word, to leave nothing but what is necessary, or at least convenient, is very difficult.

The first *Schetse* of a Comedy calld the P*aradox,* which has never seen the Light, was five times as long as the whole when it was finished; and yet were I to review it, I make no doubt, of making more Weeds, and make it yet shorter. In my opinion, the wittiest Paragraf in Monsieur *Voitures* Letters, which are all written with a great deal of Spirit, and Humour, is the Apology he makes for a long Letter, 'tis to this sense: *Pray Sir excuse the length of this, for I had not sufficient time to write a shorter*: Than which, nothing can be better and more agreeable. The same Rule is good in Books, as well as Letters; a little time is enouf to write a great Book, as they go now, and a great deal, not too much, to write a little one as it should be: Tho I am sensible this Chapter is too long, yet the next will be longer.

CHAP.

CHAP. XXI.

A Digression containing some Criticisms.

THIS Chapter is guilty of great Crimes, which it would be no small folly in me to conceal: First, it is too long, and secondly, which is worse, 'tis a Digression upon a Digression. I esteem my self obligd to declare this to the Reader, at the Threshold, before he enters into the Chapter, to the intent, that if he pleases, he may pass it over, as a long Parenthesis, and proceed to the next. But, if notwithstanding this Caution, he will be so hardy, or curious, to read it, and afterwards shall not like it, let him blame himself, not me, for I honestly set up a Beacon to prevent his splitting upon this Rock. I presume, it will be objected, Since you knew its faults, why did you publish it? I answer, Not so much to trouble others, as to ease my self, and rid my hands of it. For I am not now in circumstances to get it Companions, or Play-fellows, as I once intended, being become impotent by the loss of my Tools,

my

my Books they being all burnt by that
sudden Fire, which broke out with irresist-
able violence, after Midnight, in *Lombard-
street, Nov.* 18. *A. D.* 1693. Neither can I
endure to keep it at home alone, and hear
it eternally bawling for Liberty, like a Cat
pent up in a close Room; and besides, I
am not without hopes, there may be found
some few, to whom this will not appear so
very much disagreeable. Mr. *Hill,* to whose
account of Dr. *Barrows* Life I have so frequent recourse, says, he was addicted to
Poetry, and well skilld therein, but that he
never wrote any Satyrs; to which I add,
that the greatest part of his Poems were written in Hexameter and Pentameter Verses,
after the manner of *Ovid,* whom he had in
great esteem, preferring him even before the
Divine *Virgil:* I have heard him say, that
he believd *Virgil* could not have made the
Metamorfosis so well as *Ovid* has. Concerning which, there have been often betwixt
us several sharp, but not bitter Disputes;
for herein I confess, I differd from him,
tho we were, as to all other things, generally speaking of the same mind, as *Horace*
says of his Friend *Fuscus Aristius,* and himself.

———*Hac*

————*Hac in re, scilicet una,*
Mutum dissimiles, ad cætera, pene Gemelli,
Fraternis animis, quicquid negat, alter, & alter,
Annuimus pariter, veteres notique Columbi.

That is,
In all things else, we two, the same course steerd,
Like Doves, whom long acquaintance had endeard
Only, in this, we disagreed.

It is next to an impossibility, to write
either good Sense, or Latin, in that sort of
Metre, wherein so many hobling Dactyls
knock one against another. How often has
Martial *Pontice, Pontiliane, crede mihi,* and
innumerable such botches, forcd to the use
of them by writing thus in Shackles. Well
fare *Horace,* who amongst all his variety of
Verse, never split upon this Rock. It cannot be denied, but that *Ovid* had Wit, and
a fluent negligent Stile, an easie way of
making Verses, which, as he says, dropt
from his Pen, when he thought not of them.
Quicquid conabar dicere, Carmen erat. That
is, *Whatever I endeavour to speak, falls into
a Verse without my designing it.* He could
make a hundred Verses, *Stans pede in uno,*
while he stood upon one Foot, but either he
wanted

wanted Judgment or Patience to File and Correct them. It is recorded of him, that his Judgment was good, that he knew his Faults, but he was enamourd of them, and would not part with them: I have read this Passage, but I cannot tell where, wanting Books to have recourse to. The Story, as well as I remember it, is this: *Ovid* shewed a Copy of his Verses to some of his learned Friends, desiring their impartial Censure of them. Upon perusal they approvd them all, except one, which they desird him to alter. He replied, he would be ruld by them, and mend any Verse they should except against, but one, which he had such a kindness for, that he could by no means part with it; which was this.

Semivirumque Bovem, Semibovemque Virum.

This was the Verse which his Friends had unanimously pitchd upon, to be erasd or reformd. Add to this, *Ovid* generally stumbles at the Threshold, which is a sign of ill Luck, and shuffles like a Jade, before he can get into his right goings, beginning most of his Books ill. His *Metamorfosis* begins thus: *In nova fert Animas mutatas dicere formas,*

formas, Corpora. That is, *I intend to discourse of new Bodies, in changd forms,* instead of *Bodies changd into new forms.* This is not at all mended, by the Grammarians making it a Figure; if it is a Figure, 'tis such a one that a School-Boy would deserve whipping for imitating. His Book *De Tristibus* begins thus:

Parve, nec invideo, sine me liber ibis in Urbem,
Hei mihi quod Domino non licet ire tuo.

Here I demand, if he had envied his little Books Voyage to *Rome,* and *sed* had been the second word in the first Verse, in the place of *nec,* would not the short Verse been as much, or more to the purpose then, than it is now. Which of these two Sentences is most agreeable to Reason? *Little Book, thou art going to* Rome *without me, I envy thee not, yet I account my self the most miserable Man in the World, because my Circumstances will not permit me to accompany thee.* Or this: *Little Book, thou wilt shortly see* Rome, *and the Court of* Augustus, *from which I am for ever banisht; I envy this happiness, and cannot sufficiently lament my Condition, which makes it impossible for me to*
bear

bear thee Company. Ovids Art of Love begins thus:

Si quis, in hoc, Artem, populo non novit Amandi
  Me legat, & lecto Carmine, doctus erit.

What heinous Crime has *Artem* committed, that deservd clapping into *Little-Ease,* betwixt *hoc* and *populo* the Bark and the Tree. Could he have considerd but half a minute, he might have placed it more conveniently thus: *Si quis in hoc populo est, qui Artem non novit Amandi.* Or in lieu of *Artem,* he could have contented himself with an equivalent, as *Leges,* or *Methodum,* he might have shunnd that inconvenience, and the Verse would have run thus:

Si quis in hoc populo Leges, Methodum non
  novit Amandi.

I am also much offended at that frivolous definition, or description of the *fluctus decumanus,* or the *tenth Wave,* in these words: *Posterior nono est, undecimoque prior.* That is, *That Wave which is after the ninth, and before the eleventh.* Nothing can be more ridiculous, for this Character, *mutatis mutandis,* will

will fit indifferently all the Waves in the
Ocean, except the first; for the second is,
after the first, and before the third; the third
is, *after the second, and before the fourth*
and so on for ever. This Problem of *Ovid,
What number is betwixt Nine and Eleven*,
is much easier, than that wherewith young
Arithmeticians usd to be confounded. *If
a Herring and a half cost three Halfpence,
how many are there for a Peny?* I shall
mention but two Distichs more, and then,
having made a short visit to the *Metamorfosis*, conclude this Digression. The Verses
are these:

(sunt,

Temporibus medicina juvat, data, tempore pro-
Et data non apto tempore, vina nocent.
Utendum est ætate, cito pede præterit ætas,
Nec bona tam sequitur, quam bona prima fuit.

Who can endure *temporibus* signifying *ali-*
quando, and the nauseous repetition of the
same word thrice in two Verses. The second long Verse is subject to the same Objection, but the short one is intolerable;
yet methinks I am so well acquainted with
Ovids Humour, that he would not have
been

been prevaild with to alter it, if he had made it thus:

Nec sequitur bona tam, prima fuit bona quam.

Horace will not allow those Verses to be good, whose words being rendred in Prose, do not sound well: Whoever therefore takes the pains to bring these to that touch, and compare them with these, or almost any other of *Horace*, will find them to differ as much as Chalk and Cheese.

> ———*Aventem qui rodit Amicum,*
> *Qui non defendit, alio culpante, solutos,*
> *Qui captat risus hominum, famamq; dicacis,*
> *Fingere qui non visa potest, commissa tacere,*
> *Qui nequit, hic niger est.*

Ovids Metamorfosis has fewer Faults than the rest of his Works, but is not wholly exempt; I shall at present take notice but of three or four. In his description of the Chaos, that Hemystich, *Sine pondere, habentia pondus*, is improper, and absurd, and to be understood, must be thus filld up: *Corpora habentia pondus*, pugnabant cum iis quæ erant *sine pondere*: Or thus; *Corpora quæ e-*
rant

rant sine pondere *pugnabant cum iis quæ erant* habentia pondus. Tis evident that every Body, considerd absolutely and by it self, is heavy, that is, in *Ovids* Frase, *pondus habet*; and being compard with another Body that is more heavy, it is comparatively light, but not *sine pondere*, that it *weighs nothing*. This Sentence then thus sifted, amounts to this: *Every body fought with no Body: Impar congressus, a very unequal Battle*.

The next place I shall take notice of, is in the description of the Conflagration of the Earth, causd by *Faetons* ill management of the Horses of the Sun. Tis palpable that therein the Suns Diurnal and Annual Motion are confounded: For *Faeton* desird to drive the Chariot but for one day, as it appears by this Testimony of *Ovid* himself.

Currus petit ille paternos,
Inq; diem Alipedum jus & moderamen equorum.

And yet he is told by *Febus*, who ought to know his Trade better, that he must pass by all the Signs, and so make the Sun finish his annual Course, and produce the four Seasons of the Year in twenty four hours, which

which requires three hundred sixty five days, and some hours, minutes, and seconds more; and consequently, taking one day with a-nother, the Sun does not move one degree in twenty four hours. But some may re-ply, This is a Fault against Astronomy, not Poetry. I answer. That does not mend the matter, for a Poet ought to be a tho-row-pacd Scholar, or at least have so much discretion, as not to meddle with Sciences he understands not. He should have been mindful of that Rule, or Axiome of *Horace*: *Scribende recte, sapere est, & Principium, & Fons.* That is, *No Fool, or ignorant Persons, can Write well.* Now I reason thus; Either *Ovid* knew this Fault, or not; if he did not, then he is to be blamd for his Ignorance: If he did, and presumd that his fine descrip-tions of the terrible Beasts in the Zodiac would cast a mist before the Readers Eyes, and hinder them from taking notice of it, then is he guilty of Vanity and Presumpti-on. I shall not insist upon his description of the Galaxy, or Milky Way, which is in these words:

Est via sublimis, Cælo manifesto sereno,
Lactea nomen habet, splendore notabilis ipso.

Tis

Tis evident that *Lactea* ought to be in the same Case with *Nomen*; but I believe the Chain of his Thoughts, if he did think, was this, he would have said *Dicitur*, or *Vocatur*, but it would not serve in the Verse: Then it came into his mind, that *nomen habet*, and *Vocatur* were tantamount, and so down it goes, without minding the Solocism; whereas had he made the Verse thus, he might have shunnd it.

Nomen habens à lacte, & lactis nota colore.

I am apt to believe, that *Juvenal* usd the same way of Hunting, when he caught the word *Septem* and made use of it, when almost any other Number would have served as well.

Tunc Duas una Sævissima Vipera Cæna,
Tunc Duas? Septem si Septem forte fuissent.

That is, *Cruel Viper, what, eat two at a meal!* *yes more:* How many? Then he counts upon his Fingers, three, four, five, six, seven, that will do, go Boy write it in my Book, then down goes *Septem*, which if he had chanced to have skipt, he must have

run

run on to a hundred, before he could find
one fit for his purpose, and a hundred *Centum* would have done as well as *seven
Septem*. So the same Poet in another place:

———*Digitis à morte remotis,*
Quatuor aut Septem, *si sit latissima Tæda.*

That is, verbatim; *If it be a very broad
Torch, removd from death four or seven Inches.*
Not to mention the harshness of the Me-
tafor, a *Torch* for *a Plank*, or the impropri-
ety, of using *breadth* for *thickness*. Men
in a Ship, cannot be properly said to be
distant from death, or drowning, by the
breadth, but by the thickness of the Planks
and who ever heard of Boards seven Inches
thick? But if they exceed four, the necessity to make them fit to do service in Verse,
requires they must either be seven, or a
hundred. Notwithstanding what is here
said, I would not by any means, have it
thought that I despise either of these Poets,
nor that I could make better Verses, than
even these upon which I Criticize, this I have
done only to divert my self and the Reader,
not to diminish their Reputation. It cannot

o

not be denied they were both great Men, especially *Ovid*, his *Metamorfosis* is a Noble Piece, the Language Lofty and Elegant, it contains many excellent Descriptions, and pathetical Orations, and the Connexion of the Fables is admirable; yet I would not have him equalizd, much less preferrd to the Divine *Virgil*. *Ovid*, I confess, says, that he intended to have mended his *Metamorfosis*, but he deferrd it till it was too late: It should have been done whilst he was in *Rome*, and Prosperity; had he done it then, he might have been a formidable Competitor with *Virgil* for the Crown of Bays; but when he went into Exile, he left his Wit behind, as appears by his Book *De Tristibus*. This was the difference betwixt these two Poets; *Ovid* could never begin, and *Virgil* make an end of Correcting; as appears by his ordering his *Eneads* to be burnt: So that tis evident they did not please him, tho then brought to the perfection wherein we now have them, and they had been consumd to Ashes, to the irreparable loss of the Learned World, had not *Augustus* opportunely interposd his Soveraign Authority, and dispensed with the

Testamental

Testamental Laws, as appears by those Verses:

Quin pereat potius legum veneranda potestas,
&c.

Ovid says he burnt his *Metamorfosis* when he left *Rome*, but finding he could not wholly stifle it, there being many Copies thereof in several hands, he was willing it should live, and have six Verses, which he mentions, prefixd before it, they are in the First Book *De Tristibus*; but hear him speak in his own words:

Hos quoq; sex Versus, in prima Fronte Libelli,
Si proponendos esse putabis, habe.

That is,

All you who have my Book, if you think fit,
I'th Front cause these six Verses to be writ.

The Verses are these.

Orba Parente suo, Quicunque volumina Cernis,
   His saltem vestra detur in Urbe locus.
Quoq; magis faveas, non sunt hæc edita ab ipso,
   Sed quasi de domino funere rapta sui.
Quicquid in his igitur vitii, rude carmen habebit,
   Emendaturus, si licuisset, eram.

Which

Which may be thus made English
If these poor Orfan Books at Rome *appear,*
Make them a hearty Welcome, and good Chear.
They much impatience to get loose, exprest,
And would not stay till they were better drest;
Till I, at least, their greater faults had mended,
Which, had I livd, I faithfully intended.

Or these, out of the Third Book, which
will serve as well.
Sunt quoq; mutatæ, ter quinq; volumina formæ,
Carmina de Domini funere rapta sui.
Illud opus potuit, si non prius ipse perissem,
Certius à summa nomen habere manu.
Nunc incorrectum Populi pervenit in ora,
In Populi quicquam si tamen ore mei est.

In English thus.
Stories of Men and Gods, into strange shapes
Transformd, the better to conceal their Rapes;
Which I, at Rome, *in fifteen Books compild,*
Whilst Fortune, and Augustus *on me smild:*
Now uncorrect through many hands they move,
If many yet, poor banisht Ovid *Love.*

Both which Copies are indifferent; so much
does Adversity depress the Spirits of those,
who stand not upon the sure basis of Vertue.

To

To conclude this long, but I hope not tedious Chapter: All Ages, and Countries, even ours, might produce excellent Poets.

———*Si non offenderit unum,*
Quemque Poetarum, limæ labor, & mora.

That is,

If every one of them were not terrified, and discouragd, by the prospect of the great labour which they must undergo, and the length of time, which must be employd in filing and polishing.

CHAP. XXII.

Of Doctor Barrow.

ANno Domini 1672, Doctor *Wilkins* Bishop of *Chester*, departed this Life, and that eminently Learned Divine Doctor *Pearson* succeeded him, by which Promotion the Mastership of *Trinity-College* in *Cambridge* became vacant; this King *Charles* conferrd upon Dr. *Barrow*; and speaking of it afterwards, he said, he had given it to the best Scholar in *England*. Dr. *Barrow* was then the Kings Chaplain in Ordinary, and much in favour with the Duke of
Buckingham,

Buckingham, then Chancellor of the University of *Cambridge*, as also of *Gilbert* Lord Archbishop of *Canterbury*; both which were ready, if there had been any need, to have given him their assistance to obtain this Place. When the Patent for the Mastership was brought him, wherein there was a clause permitting him to Marry, as it had been made before for some of his Predecessors, he causd the Grant to be alterd, judging it not agreeable to the Statutes, from which he neither desird, nor would accept any Dispensation: Nay, he chose rather to be at the expence of double Fees, and procure a new Patent, *without the Marrying Clause*, than perpetually to stand upon his Guard against the Sieges, Batteries, and Importunities, which he foresaw that honourable and profitable Preferment would expose him to. *Imitatus Castora, qui se Eunuchum ipse facit, &c.* in this wisely imitating the *Beaver*, who knows for what he is hunted. Thus making Matrimony a forfeiture of his Preferment, it was as effectual a way to secure him from all dangers of that kind, as *Castration* it self could have been; for *Women* in this Age, *like Hens, desire only to Lay where they see Nest-Eggs.*

To

To shew his Humility and care of the College Revenue, he remitted to them the charge of keeping a Coach for his time, which they had done a long while before for other Masters. This Preferment so well bestowd, gladded the hearts, not only of the Members of that College, but of the University, and all lovers of Learning. Upon this, he left the Bishop of *Salisbury*, and was then so kind to me, that he earnestly invited me to spend one Winter with him at *Cambridge*; few Arguments were sufficient to make me yield my consent. The last time he was in *London*, whither he came, as it is customary, to the Election of *Westminster*, he went to *Knightsbridge* to give the Bishop of *Salisbury* a visit, and then made me engage my word, to come to him at *Trinity-College* immediately after the *Michaelmas* ensuing: I cannot express the rapture of the joy I was in, having, as I thought, so near a prospect of his charming and instructive Conversation; I fancied it would be a Heaven upon Earth, for he was immensly rich in Learning, and very liberal and communicative of it, delighting in nothing more, than to impart to others, if they desired it, whatever he had attaind by much time

time and study: but of a sudden all my hopes vanisht, and were melted like Snow before the Sun. Some few days after he came again to *Knightsbridge*, and sate down to Dinner, but I observed he did not eat: Whereupon I askd him, how it was with him: He answerd, that he had a slight Indisposition hanging upon him, with which he had struggled two or three days, and that he hopd by *Fasting* and *Opium* to get it off, as he had removd another, and more dangerous Sickness, at *Constantinople* some Years before. But these Remedies availd him not, his Malady provd in the event, an inward, malignant, and insuperable Fever, of which he died, *May* 4. *Anno Dom.* 1677, in the 47*th* Year of his Age, in mean Lodgings, at a Sadlers near *Charing-Cross*, an old, low, ill-built House, which he had usd for several Years: For tho his Condition was much betterd by his obtaining the Mastership of *Trinity-College*, yet that had no bad influence upon his Morals, he still continued the same humble Person, and could not be prevaild upon to take more reputable Lodgings: I may truly say, *Multis ille bonis flebilis occidit, Nulli flebilior quam mihi. It was a great loss to all good Men, but greatest to me.* He
left

left his Manuscripts, I mean his written Works, to Dr. *Tillotson*, and Mr. *Abraham Hill*, committing it to their discretion to publish which of them they should think fit. My Lord-Keeper sent a Message of Condolence to his Father, who had then some Place under him, importing, that he had but too great reason to grieve, for never Father lost so good a Son, and also that he should mitigate his sorrow upon that consideration. For want of sufficient instruction, I shall pass over in silence his Government of the University, when Vice-Chancellor, of the College, whilst he was Master, his public Exercises, his writing numerous and various Letters to procure Money for the building of the magnificent Library, &c. contenting my self to have set down some of the particulars which happened during my acquaintance with him, and now I shall here put a period to this Discourse, which for his, and mine own sake, I wish had been better performd. He was Buried in *Westminster-Abby*, where his Friends erected a Monument for him; the Bust, or half his Body in white Marble, placed upon a Pedestal of the same matter, whereon this Epitaf, composd by Doctor *Mapletoft*, is engravd.

ISAACUS

ISAACUS BARROW.

S. T. P. Carolo Secundo à Sacris.

Vir prope divinus, & vere magnus, si quid magni habent Pietas, Probitas, Fides, summa Eruditio, par modestia, Mores Sanctissimi undequaque & suavissimi, Goemetriæ Professor Londini Greshamensis, Græcæ linguæ, & Matheseous apud Cantabrigienses suos. Cathedras omnes, Ecclesiam, Gentem Ornavit. Collegium S. S. Trinitatis Præses illustravit, Factis Bibliothecæ, vere Regiæ, Fundamentis, auxit Opes, honores, & universum vitæ ambitum. Ad majora natus, non contempsit, sed reliquit sæculo. Deum, quem à teneris coluit, cum primis imitatus est, Paucissimis egendo, benefaciendo quam plurimis, Etiam posteris, quibus vel mortuus concionari non desinit Cætera, & pene majora, ex scriptis peti possunt.

Abi Lector, & *æmulare.*

Obiit iv. Die Maii, Anno Dom. MDCLXXVII Ætatis suæ XLVII.

Monumentum hoc Amici posuere.

In English thus.

This Monument was erected by his Friends,
To perpetuate the Memory of
ISAAC BARROW,
Dr. of Divinity, and Chaplain in Ordinary
To King *Charles* the Second.   ' He

' He was a Godlike, and truly great Man,
' if Probity, Piety, Learning in the highest
' degree, and equal Modesty, most holy
' and sweet Manners, can confer that Title.
' He was Professor of Geometry in *Gresham-*
' *College*, in *London*, and afterwards of the
' *Greek* Tongue, and Mathematics, amongst
' his *Cantabrigians*. An honour to all his
' Professions, the Church and Nation. He
' Illustrated *Trinity-College*, as Master, and
' augmented it, by laying the Foundation
' of a truly Loyal Library. Riches, Ho-
' nour, and all things desirable by most
' other Men, he did not contemn, but
' neglect. He imitated God, whom he had
' servd from his Youth, in wanting few
' things, and doing good to all, even to
' Posterity, to whom, tho dead, he yet
' Preaches. The rest, and if it is possible,
 ' greater things than these, may be
  ' found in his Writings,
 ' Go Reader, and imitate him.
He died the 4*th*. of *May*, in the 47*th*.
 ' Year of his Age, and of our
  ' Lord 1677.

CHAP.

CHAP. XXIII.

Of the Bishops Enemies.

THO they who have many Friends, have usually also many Enemies; yet this was not the Bishops lot, for never any Person in his station was more universally belovd. Amongst his Enemies, I shall not reckon the Dissenters, for their Enmity was rather against his Function than his Person; and long before his Death, as all Prosecution against them ceasd, so did their Animosities also. The Dean of *Salisbury* stirrd up a Faction against him, taking the advantage of a great, and almost total decay of his Reason; with him some of the Prebends took part, of whom the Bishop deservd a better Treatment; these flock of *Hares* had the boldness to insult, and pull by the *Beard* the dying, or rather dead *Lion*. But this Storm was soon laid, and the Bishop vindicated in hs Rights, by an Arch-Episcopal Visitation, as we shall shew hereafter.

After the Bishops death, one *Anthony A. Wood*

Wood of *Merton-College* in *Oxford*, took the liberty in his *Athenæ Oxonienses*, to use him very irreverently, as he had done many other worthy Persons, whom it is needless for me to particularize. Tis an easie thing for a melancholy Monkish Scholar, to sit in his Study, to invent and write Calumnies against whom he pleases; but the best of it is, the Dirt which he has thrown against the Bishop, is easily washt off, and that without leaving any stain. But supposing all that he says there against him to be true, it amounts but to very little, so little, that I should not have thought it worthy of my taking notice, had I not been desird by some of the Bishops surviving Friends. The summ of what he objects against him is, in short, this; *That he was a Complyer during the Kings Exile; That he put in, and put out; That after the Kings return, he boasted of his Loyalty.* As to the first; Tis true, from his coming to *Oxford* he livd peaceably, as Mr. *Wood* himself did, and the rest of the Scholars of the University, but he was far removd from any base complyance; he never was admitted a Member of the Presbyterians, Independents, or any seperated Congregation; he never frequented

quented their Meetings, never pretended
to be, or desird to be reputed against Monarchy in the Right Line, or Episcopacy,
as it was notorious to all, and as we have
made appear in the former parts of this
Book.

The second Accusation is, that he *put in
and put out:* What he means by *putting in*,
I confess I know not, neither have I ever
heard of any Person in that time, he put
in to any Place: As to the other Clause
of *putting out*, I suppose he means Mr. *Greaves*
and Dr. *Potter*. To which take this answer:
The Bishop of *Salisbury* never had but two
Places in *Oxford*, in which he succeeded
the Persons above written: How he obtaind the *Savilian* Astronomy Professorship,
or rather, how it was forced upon him,
we have truly and amply deliverd in the
third Chapter; where it appears, he did
not turn out Mr. *Greaves*, as it is here ma-
litiously insinuated. As to his being President of *Trinity-College*, after Mr. *Hawes* had
resignd, he was chosen by the Suffrages of
the Fellows, who had a legal Authority to
Elect, neither can he, by accepting of this
Place, be truly accounted to put Dr. *Potter*,
who was Ejected by the Visitors many
Years

Years before, as we have declard in the
seventh Chapter, or so much, as to keep
him out; for he was, as the Times went
then, uncapable of being Elected, and of
enjoying it, if he had been chosen. As to
the last part of his Accusation; *His boasting
of his Loyalty to the King and Church, after
his Majestys Restoration.* Why might he not
glory in a laudable Action, and a Matter of
Truth? For, as we have made it appear in
the second Chapter, he was an Actor, and
great Sufferer in that Good Cause.

Mr. *Wood* had for a long time usd the liberty to revile and speak disrespectfully of
several Eminent Persons, movd thereunto,
either by a private *pique*, or to please some
others, who lookd upon their Promotion
with an Evil Eye; this I say he had done
for a long time, with Impunity, but Vengeance, or Punishment, at last, tho late,
overtook him: It cannot be said of him,
Distulit in seram, commissa piacula mortem;
that is, *He went to his Grave unpunisht*; for
he livd to see his Book censurd and burnt,
himself expelld the University, obligd to
Recant, and give security not to offend any
more in that kind; and this he underwent
for writing too lavishly concerning a Great
Man,

Man, dead long since, upon the complaints
of some of his Relations; whereof take this
Authentic Proof, as it is Registred in the
Chancellors Court at *Oxford*, and Printed by
Authority, in the *Gazette*, Numb. 2893,
from *Monday* the 31. of *July*, to *Thursday*
August 3. 1693, in these words.

Oxford, July 31. 1693.
' **O**N the 29*th*. Instant, *Anthony A. Wood*,
' was Condemnd in the Chancellors
' Court of the University of Oxford, for ha-
' ving Written and Printed in the Second
' Volume of his *Athenæ Oxonienses*, divers
' infamous Libels against the Right Honou-
' rable *Edward*, late Earl of *Clarendon*, Lord
' High Chancellor of *England*, and Chancel-
' lor of the said University, and was there-
' fore banished the said University, until
' such time as he shall subscribe such a pub-
' lic Recantation, as the Judge of the Court
' shall approve of, and give Security not to
' offend in the like nature for the future.
' And the said Book was therefore also
' decreed to be burnt before the public
' Theatre, and on this Day it was burnt ac-
' cordingly; and public Programmas of his
                                        ' Expulsion,

' Expulsion, are already affixd on the three
' usual places.

This Punishment was severe enouf, and
may warn little ones, not to provoke the
Powerful. But as to what he has written
against the Bishop of *Salisbury*, I freely for-
give him, for this reason; but before I declare it, give me leave to tell a short Story,
which I heard at *Rome*. There was heretofore in that City a famous Confessor, who
finding that Age and Infirmity had impaird
his Memory, fearing this might render him
unfit for his Profession, made use of this
Invention to remedy that defect: He had
always in readiness, when any Penitent repaird to him to Confess, a Board, and a piece
of Chalk, with which he scord their Sins,
using several Marks, according to their degrees. It happened, that one confessd he
had kild a Man. That's a great Sin, said
the Father, and made a long Chalk upon
the Trencher: After that he confessd he had
got a Bastard. Was it, said the Ghostly Father, very gravely, a Male, or Female? The
Penitent answerd, it was a Man-Child. Say
you so, replied the Priest; *A Man is Kild,
and another got in his stead, set one against
the other*, then spitting upon his Fingers,
rubs

P

rubs out the Chalk. To apply this, the reason I promised to give for my Absolving Mr. *Wood* is this; *He had written much good of the Bishop of* Salisbury, *and truly, and but a little bad, and that falsly: Set one against the other, and let it be, as if he had never done either the one, or other.* And here I should dismiss Mr. *Wood*, and close this Chapter, had I not a just cause of quarrelling with him upon mine own account, for having endeavourd to rob me of my deserved Praise, and to obscure the most glorious Action of my Life.

———— ———— ——— *Diripere Ausus*
Hærentem Capiti, multa cum laude, Coronam.

In not mentioning that famous Contestation concerning Formalities, which I have describd at large in the fifth Chapter, or my being Proctor, but out of Ignorance or Design, either of which is sufficient to ruin the Credit of an Historian, he has falsified the History; having made the Proctors *Bifield* and *Conant*, serve for the Years 1657, and 1658, which is not only notoriously untrue, but also, it thrusts my College and my self out of the *Fasti*, or the University Chronicles;

nicles; which is an intolerable grievance to Persons thirsty of Fame, and ambitious of Honour: But for our comfort, whoever consults the University Register, or the Convocation Books, will be easily and clearly convincd of the truth of what I have here asserted.

Hence I conclude, if he may not be credited in a Matter so notoriously known, and of such importance to his History, we may, with good reason, suspect the Character he gives of a Person, with whom, I firmly believe, he never had any Conversation.

C H A P. XXIV.

Of the Bishops Sickness and Death.

THE Bishop of *Salisbury* dated his indisposition of Health, from a Fever he had in *London*, in the Year 1660 which was not well cured, as we have mentioned before; he was very ill when he was to be consecrated Bishop of *Exeter*, and not without apprehension that he should not survive that Solemnity. It was a cold rainy morning

ning when I waited on him to *Lambeth* when he was to be consecrated, and he had not been out of his Chamber for some Weeks before. He went Sick to *Exeter*, and was confin'd to his Chamber a long while, yet he remitted nothing of his Study; during that time he made the *Notitiæ* of his Diocese mentioned in the ninth Chapter. But his often travelling betwixt *Exeter* and *London*, conduced much to the meliorating of his Health, and enabled him to endure his Malady, tho not wholly to subdue it. I have heard him say, that *Colds*, to which he was very subject, never accompanied him the whole Journey, but always left him before he reach'd *Salisbury*, either in his going to *London*, or returning to *Exeter*. After he was Bishop of *Salisbury*, he was seiz'd by a dangerous scorbutical Atrofy and Looseness, as we have said in the ninth Chapter, which was cured by riding; tis a very good *Recipe*, but a dear one, R℣ *caballum*, that is, *Up and ride*. After he left off this Exercise, by which he receiv'd so much good, he complain'd of a pain in his Toe, tho, I believ'd then, that the Malady was in his Head, but I found he was displeas'd at my telling him so. I went upon this reason, upon Inspecti-

on

on no Artist could tell, which Toe was faulty; nay, I have seen the Surgeons handle and squeeze it without causing him to complain. This Malady cost him many hundred pounds in Spirit of Wine, *totus ardens*, as the Chymists call it, in dry and wet Baths, Apothecaries and Surgeons, who took his Money and laught at him in their sleeves. I have often wisht him a smart fit of the Gout, having known by the experience of others, that it clears the Head, and I doubt not, but if he had arrivd to it, it might have prolongd his Life. They who are usd to this Distemper, so frequent in the Western parts of *England*, esteem every new access a renewing the Lease of their Lives. I know a Gentleman who lived in the *Close* in *Salisbury*, who told me, I am not well, nor ever shall be, till I have a fit of the Gout, and for want of it, he in a little time died. I have heard some of those Arthritic Persons say, that the Gout it self is more tolerable than the distraction in their Thoughts, and hypochondriacal Imaginations, which succeed a Fit, if the Gout does not return in a convenient time. I have also heard, that the Archbishop of *Canterbury*, I mean *Shelden*, did not only wish for the Gout, but profferd a thousand pound

to

to any Person who would help him to it; looking upon it as the only remedy for the distemper in the Head, which he feared, might in time, prove an Apoplexy, as in fine it did, and kild him. In what I come from saying, by the word Gout, which is sometimes desirable, I mean the acute Pain, collected and fixd, during the Fit, in parts remote from the Head, and Heart, as in the Fingers, Hands, Legs, and Toes.

The Bishop had an ill Memory, even when he was in his best Health, which he empaird, by committing all things to writing, and so found by experience the *Italian* Saying true.

Chi Scrive, non ha Memoria.

That is, *Writing destroys the Memory.*

If you would make a Servant good, you must trust and employ him.

He having left off all Exercises, as I said before, his melancholy Distemper and decay of Memory gaind upon him sensibly, of which I shall give you a few Instances. At the Visitation of the Church, of which I shall speak presently, he askd several times for one of the Commissioners, who sate next to him at Dinner, which was taken notice of by all the Company. When he took the Air in his Coach, which he usd to do, almost

to

to the day of his death, he has several times
said to me, Come bear me company once
more, for twill be the last time of my going
abroad; and perceiving me to smile, what,
said he, do you rejoyce to see me so ill?
No, my Lord, I replied, I should be very
sorry, if I had the same opinion of your
Health, as I perceive you have; but I have
heard these words so frequently, and doubt
not but I shall again, that they put me not
in fear. When he has been upon the Plains,
he has imagind himself so weak, that he
could neither walk, or stand upon his Legs;
then I have said, my Lord, you know not
your strength, pray be pleasd to light out of
the Coach and try; I have prevaild with
him, and he has walkd near half a mile.
He usd to be carried from one part of his
Chamber to another in a Chair; I once
went down and left him reading, and at
my return, observd several Books had been
removd from one Table to another; whereupon I askd him, whether any body had
been there since my departure: He answerd
no; but why ask you that question? Then
I replied, I congratulate your Strength, for
either you can go, or these Folio's fly, I left
them percht upon that Table, from whence
they

they are removd. But to draw to a Conclusion. Some unkind usage, which he thought he received from the Court, which we have related in the thirteenth Chapter, together with the bad prospect of the public Affairs, all things tending to Popery and Confusion, concurring with the unjust Faction in his Church, raisd by the Dean, and fomented by some of the Prebendaries, joynd with his natural Distemper, took away his Memory, almost intirely; so that for some Years before his death, he was so alterd, that he seemd only the shadow of himself. I stile this Faction Unjust, for it was judgd so by the Visitors, who condemned the Dean to beg the Bishops pardon, which I saw him do. These Visitors were, the Right Reverend Fathers in God, *Thomas* Lord Bishop of *Rochester*, my ancient Acquaintance Fellow Collegian, and ever-honoured Friend; and Dr. *Lake*, then Lord Bishop of *Chichester*, empowerd by a Commission from his Grace Dr. *Sandcroft*, then Lord Archbishop of *Canterbury*, to inspect and compose the Differences in that Church, as I have mentioned in the additions to the *Salisbury Canto*, Stanza 4. While the Bishop was in this declining condition, I gave him

a

a visit at *Knightsbridge*; he being informd I was below, sent for me, and after saying he was glad to see me, he askd me, How does your Brother? I replied, whom does your Lordship mean? He answerd, Bishop *Wilkins*, who had been dead near then fourteen Years. He attempted to speak to me again, beginning thus; Were not you surprizd *to hear, to hear, to hear*; but he could proceed no further, having, in that short time, irrecoverably forgot what he intended to have spoke. Thenceforward he continued, for it cannot be properly said he livd, almost void of Reason. I have known, at his return from taking the Air, in a very hot Summers day, the Nurse used this Argument to prevail with him to come out of the Coach; *My Lord, theres a very good Fire in your Chamber*: He did not then know his House, or his Servants; in a word, he knew nothing. I had him in my eye, when I made the fifteenth Stanza of the W I S H, which begins thus:

To out-live my Senses may it not be my Fate.
He had also strange imaginations of things which never were, and firmly believd them. One Example whereof, is too much, that one of his Servants had got so much under
him,

him, that he built a whole Street in *London*, and married a rich Lady.

Poor Gentleman, the Evil that he most feard, and I may say, even foresaw, fell upon him. He has often discoursd with me concerning some Persons, whom we both knew, and who were thus decayd, and became the Properties of those who first seizd on them, who kept them to their selves, made their Wills, and disposd of their Estates as they thought fit. *If you ever see me in such dangers*, said he, *pray give me warning*; but his decay was so precipitous, that twas impossible to relieve him. This sad Story would afford many useful Corollaries, which I leave to the Reader to find out, and apply.

To conclude, he died *January* 6. *Anno Dom.* 1683, knowing nothing of the Revolution that had happened. He was carried from *Knightsbridge* to *Salisbury*, and buried in the place, which, he and I, had long before concerted, and agreed on, as I have deliverd in the ninth Chapter. His Nevew Mr. *Seth Ward*, has erected a Monument for him, with a Latin Inscription, which I once resolved to have omitted, for it is long, and erroneous; but upon second considerations,

I

I thought my self obligd to Copy and Translate it, that there might be nothing wantin this Account.

CHAP. XXV.

The Bishops Epitaf in Latin.

H. S. E.

REverendus in Christo Pater, Sethus Ward, *Ecclesiæ Sarisburiensis Episcopus, & Nobilissimi Ordinis, à Periscelide dicti, Cancellarius, Ab Ecclesia Exoniensi (in qua etiam Præcentor primum, deinde Decanus fuerat) in hanc sedem translatus, in utraque æternum colendus.*

Buntingfordiæ, in Agro Hertfordiensi natus, Cantabrigiæ in Collegio Sidneiensi educatus, ejusdemque (dum per temporum iniquitatem licuit) socius. In tam privata sortis umbra, tot optimarum Artium, virtutumque dotibus effulsit, ut frustra latere cupientem, prodiderint, inque lecem simul, & utilitatem publicam protaxerint.

Quippe ab ista Academia, ad alteram Oxoniensem evocatus, Astronomiæ primum. Professor Savilianus, Collegii deinde Sacro Sanctæ Trinitatis Præses electus, ambo, licet dispavis

ingenii

ingenii munia, sapientia administravit & pru-
dentia pari, Siderum, simul & animarum, In-
dagator perspicax, & in amborum motibus re-
gendis, vigilans, peritas, fœlix. Prælectionum
suarum famam qua claruerit foris, testatur
Bullialdus. Adversus, insaniam & impiam Fi-
losofiam, quid meruerit domi, abunde sensit, pri-
mipilus Hobbius, contra ingruentem Fanatico-
rum barbariem quid literis ubique præstiterit,
vindicatæ agnoscunt Academiæ. Hæres per in-
quissima tempora, tam præclare gestæ, probatum
satis, & bene præparatum, meliore jam rerum
vice, hominum & ingeniorum peritissimo judici
Carolo Secundo, commendarunt, ut secum restau-
randis Ecclesiæ Anglicanæ ruinis, non Erube-
scendus opifex allaborarit, ut prudentia, pietate,
usu rerum, & præcipue moderato animo spectabi-
lis, Civium æstus, nondum bene sedatos, compo-
neret, inveterata ulcera leniret, concionator fa-
cundus, & potens, inculpabile gregis Exemplar,
mox & Pastorum futurus, siquidem per hos la-
borum & meritorum gradus, ad Episcopale cul-
men provectus Ecclesiæ suæ Candelabrum, ip-
samque domum Dei, non impari lumine imple-
vit, & illustravit. In officiis erga omnes, cujus
cunque sortis & Ordinis homines exequendis,
æqui & decori observantissimus, cum confratri-
bus, & Dominis suis Episcopis, inviolata con-
cordia,

cordia, absque omni, (*nisi mutuo benefaciendi*) *certamine semper vixit. Apud Clerum suum, tanquam fratres, & filios dilectissimos, autoritate & reverentia, non metu, aut fastu dignitatam Prælati illibatam conservavit. Nobiles, & Cives, munificentia, domesticos liberali tractatione, devinxit. In asserendis Ecclesiæ juribus, ut vindex acerrimus, ita nec deses in suis, Cancellariatum Periscelidis, sedis suæ antiquum decus, postquam per CL. circiter annos, penes Laicos subsedisset, secundum vindicias sibi postulavit, & recepit. Palatii Episcopalis, largus, & Sedulus Instaurator, nec minus erga Templum munificus, sed præcipua, & palmaria illi fuit Pauperum cura, in hac, neque metas, neque terminos, aut vivens, aut moriens pietati suæ præscripsit.* Subsidum sine fine parans.

Buntingfordiæ, Cænobium quatuor Viris totidemque feminis copioso, & honesto, apparatu instructum fundavit. Cantabrigiæ, in Collegio Christi, sex Scholarium numero, æquo jure, & Privilegio cum cæteris gaudentium, pristinam fundationem adauxit.

In hac Urbe, Collegium Decem Presbyterorum viduis, Apostolico ritu instituit, primitiva munificentia donavit. Hæc omnia agentem, & peragentem, Senectus primum deinde mors, utra-
que

*que pariter tranquilla, pariter matura, præ-
munitum, & præparatum, occuparunt.*

$$Anno \begin{cases} \textit{Ætatis suæ LXXII.} \\ \textit{Translationis XXII.} \\ \textit{Æræ Christianæ MDCLXXXIII.} \end{cases}$$

*I, Lector, & plures illi similes operarios,
huic Vineæ apprecare.*

CHAP. XXVI.

The Epitaf in English.

THis good Bishop deservd a better E-
pitaf, this is heavy, long, and tedious, but being sifted, and garbled, it may
be thus rendred into English, *viz.*

' Here lies the Reverend Father in God,
' *Seth Ward*, Bishop of *Salisbury*, and Chan-
' cellor of the most Noble Order of the Gar-
' ter. He had been successively, Chanter,
' Dean, and Bishop of *Exeter*, from whence
' he was translated unto this Diocese.

' He was Born at *Buntingford* in *Hertford-
' shire*, Educated at *Cambridge*, and Fellow
' of *Sidney College*, till thence ejected, for re-
' fusing the Covenant. Afterwards he re-
' movd

' movd to *Oxford*, whence he was, first *Sa-*
' *vilian* Professor of Astronomy, and after-
' wards President of *Trinity College*. In the
' execution of both those Places, he gave
' ample testimony of his Learning and Pru-
' dence, and gaind great Reputation. Du-
' ring his abode at *Oxford*, he wrote against
' *Bullialdus*, and Mr. *Hobbs*, as also a Vin-
' dication of the Universities, in reply to
' one *Webster* of *Cletherow*, who had writ
' a Pamflet to prove them useless. The
' Fame of his Learning, his Eloquent and
' powerful Preaching, his experience, and
' ability for Business, causd King *Charles*
' the Second to take notice of him, and
' make him a Bishop, and to use his assi-
' stance in repairing the ruins of the Church,
' to which he was an Ornament and Sup-
' port. With his Brethren the Bishops, he
' had no other Contention, but striving
' which of them should do most good.
' With the Clergy of his Diocese, he livd
' as a prudent and affectionate Father a-
' mongst his Children, and with his Pater-
' nal Authority, not by his Pride and
' Haughtiness, conservd the Episcopal Dig-
' nity inviolable. He drew to himself the
' love of all, by his Liberality, Hospitality,
                                    ' affable,

' affable, humble, chearful, and obliging
' Conversation.

' He was at vast Expence in rebuilding
' his Palace, in repairing and beautifying
' the Cathedral.

' He was a zealous and successful Asser-
' tor of the Rights of the Church, as ap-
' pears by his recovering the Chancellor-
' ship of the Garter, and getting it annex-
' ed to the Bishops of *Salisbury* for ever, af-
' ter it had been in Lay hands about a hun-
' dred and fifty Years.

' His greatest care was for the Poor,
' whom he not only liberally fed in his Life,
' but provided for also after his Death.

' At *Christs College* in *Cambridge*, he In-
' stituted six Scholarships, enjoying the
' same Privileges with those of the old
' Foundation.

' At *Buntingford* he built an Hospital for
' four poor Men, and as many Women,
' and endowd it with a competent Mainte-
' nance.

' In this City he erected the College of
' Matrons, and generously endowd it with
' a comfortable subsistance for Ten Widows
' of Orthodox Clergymen. Old Age and
' Death seizd on him, thus doing, and found
' him

'him forewarnd, and prepard: He died
'in the Seventy second Year of his Age,
'the Twenty second of his Translation,
'and in the Year of our Lord, 1688.

   'Go, Reader, pray that more such La-
'bourers may be sent into the Vineyard.

C H A P. XXVII.

The Conclusion.

IF you tell an *Italian*, such a one is vast-
ly Rich, his usual reply is, *Dam mi lo
morto:* that is, *It will appear at his death
whether he be or not.* *Ovid*, not without
reason, enlarges the time, in these words:

—————————*Dicique beatus,*
Ante obitum nemo, supremaq; funera debet.

That is, *No Man ought to be accounted happy,
before he is dead and buried.* So *Petrarch,*

Il Giorno, la sera, la vita, loda il Fine.
That is, *Call not the day fair, wherein it rains
before Sun-set; Nor that life happy, which does
not end well.*

                                  I

I should have accounted this Bishop of *Salisbury* invidiously happy, had his *Exit* been answerable to his glorious *Acting* upon the *Stage* of the World: Had he either died sooner, or lived longer, I mean, had he died before that great, I may say, Total decay of his Senses and Reason befel him, or livd with them intire, *Integra cum mente*, to have born his share, and added one more to the number of those Faithful Bishops, whose Imprisonment, Tryal, and Deliverance, ought never to be forgotten, had he livd to have seen those Clouds blown over, the Church and Civil Rights of *England* restord and securd.

Jamque Opus exegi————

Altho I do not pretend to what follows:

————*quod nec Jovis Ira, nec Ignis,*
Nec poterit ferrum, nec Edax abolere vetustas.

Yet, I believe, this Book will be longer livd than the Author, and that I shall be consumd by *Worms*, before the *Moths* shall have devoured it. I have, I say, finisht the Task I imposd upon my Self, as to the Performance, the Readers will be Judges, according to their Capacities and Inclinations;

tions; but if they pronounce Sentence against me, I have this to hold up my Spirits, that I am certain, *No Man could have written this Life better, or so well, without my assistance.*

Now one word to thee, my little Book, if the Fanatics rise up in Arms and assault thee;

Tu ne cede malis, sed contra Audentior ito.
That is, *Let not thy noble Courage be cast down.*

Fight it out to the last drop of Blood, never yield, never beg Quarter, for they will give thee none, for having spoken well of a Bishop. Let this be thy comfort, the more they rail against thee, the more despitefully they use thee; thou shalt be so much the more in my favour, and I shall think it a sufficient reason to believe, that there is something good in thee, whereat they are so much offended.

And now I have no more to say of the Bishop of *Salisbury*, and only this concerning my Self. I thank God for prolonging my days, till I have given the World this public Testimony of my Gratitude; and here, without begging the Reader to be be Courteous, or making Apologies for my Stile, for my long, frequent, and, as they will be thought by some, impertinent Digressions, I shall conclude with those Verses of *Imperiale*.

————————Meglio Amo,
Al mondo tutto Dicitor mal saggio,
E scarso d' Arte, è d' alto Stil mendico,
Che, à te solo parer, non grato Amico.

Which may be thus Translated,

I had rather the whole World should say of me,
My Stile is flat and trivial, theres no Wit,
Nor one grain of good Sense in all I have writ,
Then seem ungrateful, blessed Saint, to thee.

Liberavi Animam meam Domine nunc dimittis.

I have disingaged my Soul, I have paid my Debt to my deceased Friend, I am, I thank God, arrivd to a good Old Age, without *Gout* or *Stone*, with my External Senses, but little decayd, and my Intellectuals, tho none of the best, yet as good as ever they were. *Lord, now dismiss thy Servant in Peace, according to thy Word.*

·*F I N I S.*